MAGIC TRICKS

MAGIC TRICKS

Keith Fields

Dedication

To the three people who mean the most to me.
Sarah, my patient and ever loving wife.
Matthew, the best son a father ever had.
And the bump that is not yet born.

Acknowledgements

The author wishes to thank Danny Edwards for
appearing in some of the photos, Michael Plomer,
probably the best photographer in the world, Brian
Trodd for not moaning when the book was late, Tony
Truscott for taking my pile of pictures and words and
turning them into this beautiful book. Thanks also to
the team at Regency House Publishing Ltd., who for
some reason think I am the best magician in the
world. And Simon Lovell who said he'd never talk to
me again if he didn't get a mention!

Published in the USA by JG Press
Distributed by World Publications, Inc.

The JG Press imprint is a trademark of JG Press, Inc.
455 Somerset Avenue
North Dighton, MA 02764

**Copyright © 1995 Regency House
Publishing Limited**

ISBN 1-57215–100–5

Printed in China.

Contents

Descriptions of tricks are given as performed by the author, who happens to be right-handed. Left-handed readers may prefer to transpose all directions to the opposite hand.

Introduction

Anyone can be a magician. This book has been written to start you, the reader, on the trail of an interesting and absorbing hobby, a hobby which can, with practice, become a lucrative occupation. Magic is not an easy subject to learn about: the secrecy and intrigue tied up with the art, and carefully maintained by its masters, make it hard to become a magician – hard, but not impossible.

Magicians argue: You want to be a magician, but you don't know any tricks. Ask a magician to help and he will say "I cannot teach you any tricks because you are not a magician."

"If everyone knew how the tricks were done there would be no magic, therefore we must absolutely keep our methods secret."

But if magicians keep all their methods secret and maintain their mystery then there will be no new young magicians, and soon there will be no magic.

It is a circular argument. Is there no way in?

Well, you study the contents of this book, learn the moves and methods explained, and actually start performing. This book is the key which can unlock the door to a whole new world.

Anyone can be a magician. It takes hard work and dedication to become highly skilled in a chosen area. A great golfer will commit his whole life to golf; it will affect his diet, his social life, his work, his thoughts, it will fill most of his days, but you do not need to be that single-minded to enjoy playing golf. Magic is much the same. If you want to be the best then you must do nothing else, but it can be, and indeed is, a great hobby for thousands of people all over the world. You do not need to be a special person, you do not need special gifts, you just need the willingness to learn.

So where do you start? Here, and now, read on and find the type of tricks which interest you. Learn and practise them. You will then have to think about how and where to perform the tricks, and when you have crossed those barriers, you are already well on your way to becoming a first-class entertainer.

Magic should be fun, so learn the tricks well and enjoy them. Who knows, one day you might be the next David Copperfield.

SOME RULES

NEVER EXPOSE THE METHOD OF MAGIC

Under no circumstances tell your audience how the tricks are done. Without mystery there is no magic: it is secrecy which keeps magic alive. You may think it is all right to let someone know how just one small trick is done, perhaps one that you do not perform yourself, but it is not. After all, if all magicians did this our secrets would no longer be secrets, and you would no longer have an interesting hobby.

NEVER BORE PEOPLE WITH MAGIC

You will find that people do not want to see the same trick over and over again, and will not want to pick a card for the eighty-third time today. If you repeat a trick you may give enough away for your audience to work out the method – this is as foolish as giving away secrets. It is worth bearing in mind the old show business saying "leave them wanting more". How many tricks should you show someone? Answer: one less than they want to see! Your object must always be to entertain. This will develop an interest in magic from your audience, rather than encourage them to avoid you!

NEVER PERFORM A TRICK THAT IS NOT THOROUGHLY REHEARSED

If you make a mistake in a trick you will be giving away the method. When you learn a new routine study everything carefully so that you know what could possible go wrong. Anything that can go wrong will go wrong – usually when you are doing a crucial audition! Practise as much as possible, and do not perform a new trick until you feel completely confident with it.

ALWAYS ENJOY YOUR MAGIC

The one thing that will sell your tricks more than anything else is the fact that your are enjoying them yourself. If you feel very tense or nervous the audience will also be on edge. If you relax, then they will relax and enjoy themselves too.

CARD MAGIC

Card games have been played in Europe for over five hundred years and card tricks have been around for almost as long. They were included in the first magic book called *The Discoverie of Witchcraft* by Scott, published in 1584, and no introductory book on magic would be complete without a section on card tricks. Many books have been written that are just about card tricks and the sheer number of tricks and the diversity of the plots is amazing, and new ideas are always being introduced.

A pack of cards can easily be kept in the pocket, giving you the ability to perform a whole act without resorting to any other props. Bear in mind though, that generally two or three card tricks in a routine are sufficient if the audience is not to lose interest. It is a good idea to break card tricks up with other effects.

Do not be put off by thinking that card tricks take incredible dexterity and hours of practice at complicated sleight of hand. Many card tricks are completely self-working and are very simple to do, but a little practice at the flourishes and learning how to handle a pack of cards will pay dividends. If the audience see you shuffling a pack and then cut it with one hand they will credit you with great skill even when you perform the simplest of card tricks!

HANDLE THE CARDS LIKE A PRO

If you are going to do card tricks then you must learn to handle the cards with confidence. It is not a good idea to try to impress someone with your sleight of hand one moment and spend the next moment picking the cards up off the floor! Learning to handle a pack of cards takes a little time and effort but you can practise while watching the television, travelling by train or in a car (assuming you're not driving!) or almost anytime your hands are free – save time by doing two things at once. You should practise dealing the cards, shuffling the cards and cutting the cards until you can do them with confidence. There are many ways of shuffling cards and we are going to start by looking at a couple that you should learn.

CARD TERMINOLOGY

BACK : The back of the card is the side with a single geometric design so that from this side they all look alike

FACE : The opposite side to the back, printed with the suit (clubs, hearts, spades, diamonds) and the value of the card

COURT OR PICTURE CARD : The jack, queen, and king

SPOT CARD : The number cards, ace through ten

STOCK : A small packet of cards that are held together in either hand

CUT THE CARDS : Lift off a stock of approximately half the pack and place it beside the lower portion

COMPLETE THE CUT : Place the lower portion on top of the upper portion that has just been cut

TOP OF THE DECK : When the deck is face down, the uppermost card or top portion of the deck of cards

BOTTOM OF DECK : The lowermost card or portion of the deck

THE OVERHAND SHUFFLE

The cards are held in the right hand and you are going to shuffle them off into the left hand. The right hand lowers the whole pack towards the left hand and the left thumb is raised to pull off a small packet of the cards. As this happens the right hand is raised taking with it the remaining stock of cards. The situation after this first move is that a small stock of approximately 10 cards are held in the left hand with the majority of the cards retained in the right hand. The next part of the move is a repeat of the above only there is a small stock of cards already in the left hand. The right hand is lowered again into the left hand where the left thumb is going to pull off another small stock of cards, note that the right hand cards are lowered into the left hand to the left of the small stock that is there from the previous stage. This action is repeated several times until you run out of cards in the right hand.

A small stock of cards is pulled into the left hand with the left thumb.

The second and subsequent moves place more cards into the left hand on top of the stock already there.

THE RIFFLE SHUFFLE

The starting position for the riffle shuffle. The slight bend in the cards is as a result of the downward pressure of the first fingers and the upwards pressure of the thumb. Do not put on too much pressure or you will find it difficult to control the riffle.

As the cards slip off the bottom of the thumbs the edges should weave together. With practice the alternate weaving of the cards from each hand will be quite accurate.

This will take a little practice but is well worth learning as it does two things, firstly it shuffles the cards and secondly, when combined with the riffle weave, it is an impressive flourish. Fun to do and pretty to watch, mastering this shuffle will impress your audience. This shuffle needs to be learnt on a table top but with practice you can do it in your hands.

Place the pack on the table so that the long edge of the cards are running parallel to the edge of the table nearest your body. Now cut off about half of the pack and place them next to the deck on the table, the short edges of the cards should be side by side and about 2cm (¾in) apart. You are going to pick up the left pile in your left hand and the right pile in your right hand. The thumbs go into the gap between the two piles and are placed in the centre of the short edge. The second, third and fourth fingers are used to grip the outer short edge of each stock of cards. The first fingers are placed on the centre of the cards. A little pressure is applied by gently pushing down with the first fingers and pulling back with the thumbs. In readiness for the next stage the two hands must be brought a little closer together so that when released the cards will weave together.

The thumbs of both hands are simultaneously pulled up a little more so that cards can trickle off the bottom of the two stocks. With practice you will learn the right amount of pressure to apply to get a smooth flow of cards from each thumb. As the cards are released they will weave with the cards from the other hand. This will not happen the first time you try this shuffle! Cards will fall from your thumbs in uncontrolled jerks, do not be put off, put in a little practice and you will soon master the technique. The cards should interlock by about 1cm (⅜in), if this is not the case then the hands should be moved apart or together to compensate.

When all the cards have been released from the thumbs you can either go on to the riffle weave or take the easier option, which is to put your hands on the outside edges of the cards and simply push them together and square the pack. Master the riffle shuffle before attempting the riffle weave.

THE RIFFLE WEAVE

If you rush into this stage before mastering the riffle shuffle then you are about to spend time picking cards up off the floor! This is not an easy move but the work that you have put in to learn the riffle shuffle is the groundwork for the riffle weave. This

Right: Ready to start the riffle weave. Note the bend in the cards which makes them want to spring up and the position of the thumbs which are holding the cards down.

Left: As the fingers are slowly moved apart the cards flow down and are squared up in-between the fingers.

move is a flashy way of completing the shuffle so that the cards are seen to weave together and square up in your hands.

The starting position for the riffle weave is the finishing position of the riffle shuffle. That is, the two stocks of cards should be on the table with the ends alternately overlapping by approximately

1cm (³⁄₈in). If as a result of a slightly sloppy riffle shuffle the cards are not squared up it is a good thing to do it now, it is not easy to do the weave if the cards are not evenly mixed and square.

The cards must be picked up without interrupting the weaving that was achieved during the riffle shuffle. The thumbs of both hands overlap on the top of the cards and the fingers are wrapped around the outside edges. The thumbs must be in place or the cards will pop up and end up all over the table. Push gently in with the fingers so that the cards bend

slightly and push up against the thumbs. As long as the cards are bent and under pressure they should stay in the position shown in the picture above. If you find that the cards do not go into the correct position you need to apply more pressure with the fingers and increase the bend in the cards.

Now comes the fun part! Slowly release the pressure on the cards by moving the fingers apart. This should result in the cards weaving down and squaring up in your hands, and making a waterfall noise in the process. The speed of this action is under your control, you should aim for a constant smooth action so that people can see the cards weaving together. If the cards are weaving too quickly then start off with more pressure (i.e. push the fingers closer together) at the start and release the pressure a little more slowly.

The first few times you try the riffle shuffle and weave will be unsuccessful, it takes practice and you have to learn to do the move by 'feel'. You will quickly learn the correct amount of pressure and bend to put into the cards so do not give up too soon. An important thing to note is that brand new cards are stiffer and springier than a used pack and can be more difficult to handle; on the other hand a used pack can be stickier and not flow freely, ideally this shuffle should be learned using a slightly worn deck. This is the hardest card move in the book so when you have mastered this then everything else contained in these pages is easily within your grasp.

THE MECHANIC'S GRIP

The Mechanic's Grip or the basic dealing position. It is important to practise dealing cards until you have a smooth and professional action. Many tricks involve the dealing out of several piles of cards and this needs to be done quickly so that the tricks do not become boring. Practise dealing both face up and face down piles of cards until you can do it without thinking.

CARD FLOURISHES

When performing card tricks it is a good thing to throw in a few flourishes with the cards. The audience are then likely to credit you with great skill even when performing a simple trick. The moves described below are not tricks, they are all moves designed to show off your skill with cards and to make you look like an expert! These moves are not as difficult as they will seem when you first try them. The first few attempts are likely to end in cards all over the floor so it is best to start practising over a table (it saves a lot of bending down and picking up!) You will find that card flourishes are easier if your hands are clean and smooth, this also keeps the cards free from grease and makes them last a lot longer. Enough about personal hygiene – pick up the cards and we'll start with the one-handed cut.

THE CHARLIER PASS

The Charlier Pass is the technical name given to this version of the one-handed cut. Like many flourishes it is a lot harder to do slowly than it is at full speed, this makes the initial learning of the move quite difficult. As soon as you have successfully completed the move with a pack in your hand and you know the correct sequence of events you should put the book down and practise the move from memory.

STAGE 1

Hold the cards between the tips of your thumb and fingers as shown. The first finger is curled under the pack in readiness for the next stage. By rolling the thumb out and away from the bottom of the pack a stock of cards will fall into the palm of your hand.

STAGE 2

With the cards in this position you will notice that there is nothing to hold the cards of the lower stock together. A slight tilt in either direction will cause the cards to slip out of your hands. When performing at full speed this problem automatically disappears but during practice you must remember to keep the bottom stock from slipping. The first finger is now used to push the bottom stock up to meet the thumb, the cards will then form a tent shape in your hand.

STAGE 3

The bottom stock is pushed up and gripped between the first finger and thumb. This causes the thumb to release its hold on the top stock. Push a little further with the finger (which should be at the apex of the tent shape) and the top stock will slip over the edge of the bottom stock and be caught on the end of the first finger in preparation for the next stage. The top stock is now loosely balanced and will slip off the hand if it is tilted.

STAGE 4

The first finger is now used to lower the top stock into the palm of the hand while the thumb holds the bottom stock in a vertical position. As soon as the top stock is horizontal the thumb pushes the bottom stock onto the top of the pack thus completing the cut. The cards can now be squared up using all the fingers, returning you to the starting position.

THE RUSSIAN SHUFFLE

This is the flourish where cards are sprung out of one hand and caught in the other (they are rushing after one another, hence the name – a dreadful pun!) The positioning of the fingers and thumbs of both hands are very important in this flourish but it will certainly get you plenty of attention when you have mastered it.

A lot of people have tried and failed at this flourish because of one little known fault: the direction of the bend in the cards at the start of the move. If the cards are bent away from your hand (convex) it will be impossible to control the direction of the flow of cards. The cards should be held with the fingers and the thumb on the opposite short edges of the cards and the bend must be towards the palm of your hand (concave). The thumb must be protruding past the edge of the deck while the tips of the fingers must be on the very edge of the deck. The cards are released by straightening the fingers slowly and letting them slip off the fingertips (never let the cards slip off the thumb end). By controlling the release of the cards, using pressure between the fingers and thumbs, you will soon be able to cause a steady flow of cards from your hand.

The catching hand is made into a cradle, the thumb and the second through little fingers form the two sides and the first finger is at the end to stop any cards overshooting. Initially, you should start with the hands almost touching. Bend the cards in the right hand and then let them slip off the fingers into the left hand. When you have managed to do this, and get an even and smooth flow of cards from one hand to the other, it is time to start separating the hands a little. After a little while you should be able to do this over a 10cm (4in) gap, the greater the distance between the hands the more the accuracy that is needed in both hands, so increase the distance slowly.

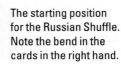

The starting position for the Russian Shuffle. Note the bend in the cards in the right hand.

The Russian Shuffle in progress. See how the left hand fingers cradle the cards and stop them falling out.

CARD FANS

This is a very pretty flourish and it always impresses an audience. Imagine taking a pack of single playing cards and with a single sweep of the thumb creating a fan so that each and every card is clearly visible. It is a good way to show that a deck is normal and well shuffled. This is impossible to do if the cards are old and sticky or if the cards are of a cheap quality. Good linen or plastic cards fan well when new, plastic cards seem to get stickier quicker so if you are buying a pack for fanning practice get linen finish. Coloured and picture backs look pretty when fanned and can be turned around to create different patterns. The fan can be used with the deck face up or face down so if you are doing a trick where a card is chosen, why not use a fan.

STAGE 1

Hold the cards in the left hand as shown. The fingers are all straight and held together to create a flat bed on which the fan is made. The cards are angled back at the start so that the largest possible fan is made. The thumb is lightly pushing down and is the pivot point for the fan.

STAGE 2

The right thumb or first finger can be used to make the fan. The action should be one clean continuous sweep with the thumb as it makes the fan shape by letting cards trickle out beneath it. Keep a light grip with the left thumb so the cards continue to pivot around the same point.

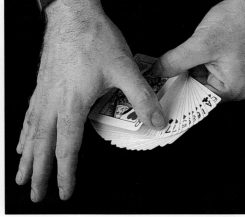

STAGE 3

Keep the sweeping action going with the thumb (or first finger) until you can go no further. The fingers of the left hand are still held as a flat bed under the fan and the thumb is pushing down to stop any cards from slipping away. With practice you can fan the cards to make three-quarters of a circle, but start small and build up to it.

As with many card flourishes the important thing is 'feel'. The amount of downwards pressure by the thumb (the pivot point) varies depending on the angle at which the cards are held and the speed of the fanning action. Spend an evening in front of the television with a pack of cards and you will soon be fanning and Charlier passing to your heart's content.

THE 21 CARD TRICK

Sometimes it is harder to explain how a trick works than how to do it and this is one of those tricks. The good news is that it is completely self-working (as are most of the tricks in this book) with no complicated moves. Just follow the instructions and the trick will work. It uses 21 cards dealt into three 'hands' of seven cards. One of the cards is selected by a spectator and after dealing the cards twice more the card is found using a magic spell.

METHOD

Take the pack of cards and deal three columns of cards with seven cards in each column. It is very important that the cards are dealt in the following way. Deal three cards onto the table, from left to right. Following the same left to right pattern place a second card on each of the three cards on the table. Repeat this process until there are three columns of seven cards on the table. The action is the same as if you were dealing three hands in a game of whist, apart from the fact that the cards are face up. Place the remainder of the pack to one side as it is not needed.

Ask the spectator to select a card. They do not need to touch it, they just need to point to the column containing their card. Gather each of the three columns into three piles of seven cards and then stack them together making sure that the column that they pointed to goes in between the other two columns.

Pick up the 21 cards and deal them out again in exactly the same way as before. Ask again which column their card is in and place that column between the other two. This process is repeated once more and the trick is done. Because of the dealing and stacking of the cards the chosen card has repositioned itself to be eleventh from the top. You could just count down to the card but I prefer to do the following. At this point in the trick I ask the audience if they know any magic words. Someone will always say 'Abracadabra' or 'Hocus Pocus', these are the most common ones and the ones to listen out for. Using the chosen magic word you are going to find their card. The card as you know is at position 11 in the stack and as Abracadabra has 11 letters simply spell it out using one card for each letter. When you get to the final 'A' that will be the selected card. 'Hocus Pocus' only has 10 letters so if using this magic word spell it out, one card for each letter, and the next card will be the selected card.

You can make up your own magic word as long as it has enough letters in it or if you know the name of the person that is watching the trick and that has either 10 or 11 letters in it then you can use that. Finding the chosen card by spelling their name will get a really good reaction.

Left: Deal the cards left to right in three columns. The column containing the selected card must go between the other two columns.

Right: Spelling out a magic word is a great way to get to the finale of the trick – maybe they do work!

THE FOUR BURGLARS

This is a nice trick because it gets away from the old 'pick a card' style. The audience see you place four jacks on top of the pack, these are then inserted one at a time into the centre of the deck but with a snap of your fingers they all re-appear back on top. This action happens as you tell a story about four burglars who break into a block of flats and escape from the police with the aid of a bit of magic. A good little story and strong magic, what more could you ask for?

METHOD

Before you perform this trick you must get ready by sorting out the four jacks. This can be done in front of the audience by running through the cards, faces towards you, and moving each jack to the front of the pack as you come across it. You now take the four jacks plus three extra cards from the deck, the audience must not see you take the extra cards so when you remove them make sure that they are all squared up. If you find this process a little difficult then prepare for the trick when the attention of the audience is on something else, only draw attention to yourself when you have the four jacks plus three different cards squared up and ready in your hands.

Hold the four jacks (plus three cards) in the Mechanic's Grip (see page 9) and pull the first three cards down with the fingers of your other hand, this is a simple action that shows the jacks without exposing the extra cards which remain hidden behind the fourth jack. Tell the story as follows: 'There were four burglars *(point to the jacks and square them up)* who decided to rob a block of flats *(point to the pack of cards)*. They decided to start at the top and work down *(place the jack stack on top of the pack)*. The first jack broke into the top flat *(put the top card, not a jack, in the top half of the deck)*. The second jack broke into the middle flat *(place the top card in the middle of the pack)*. The third jack broke into the bottom flat *(again place the top card in the pack)*. The last one stayed on top of the flats to act as a lookout *(lift the top card and show it to the audience, it is a jack)*. In the

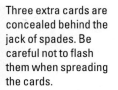

Three extra cards are concealed behind the jack of spades. Be careful not to flash them when spreading the cards.

Above: As you tell the story take the three extra cards off the top (pretending they are jacks) and place them into the middle of the pack.

Left: Quick as a flash the jacks reassemble on the top of the pack to make their escape!

distance he heard a police car and he knew that someone had tipped the police off about the robbery that was in process, so he tapped the pack three times *(suit actions to words)* and the other jacks ran up the stairs to join him and they made their escape.' *(Deal off the four jacks from the top of the pack)*.

The trick works by using the extra

secret cards behind the jacks, it is these that are placed into the centre of the pack and not the jacks, which are left on top of the pack throughout the whole trick. Make sure not to flash the faces of the other cards as you place them in the pack and the audience will think you have incredible skill as a card magician.

THE UPSIDE-DOWN CARD MYSTERY

Having a card selected and then finding it after it has been lost in the pack is the simplest form of card trick. It is also the most boring. This is a version of that trick which has a great deal more impact because the card is not only discovered but it has magically turned over in the pack. Using this method you can have three cards chosen by three people and find them all as quickly as you can blink. This involves more people in the trick and makes it more interesting for everybody.

METHOD

Before you start to perform this trick there is one simple thing to do, turn the bottom card over so that it is face up. Hold the pack in your hands so that you have 51 face down cards and beneath it the one face up card. Having done that you are ready to perform.

Spread the top half of the cards between your hands and ask someone to select a card. Make sure that you keep the bottom portion of the deck squared up in your hand so that the face up card is not seen. Square up the cards again and hold the pack in your left hand, ask the spectator who has chosen the card to show it to anyone else who is watching so that they will all be able to share the excitement of the magic that is about to happen. As you say this casually drop the hand containing the cards to your side and turn it over. When you bring your hand forward again you will have one face down card on the top of the pack and the rest of the cards are face up. No one will notice this manoeuvre as they will be looking at the card that has just been selected.

You are now going to return the card to the pack. Bring the left hand which contains the cards back up from your side and at the same time ask the spectator to give you the card face down so you will not be able to tell what it is. Take the card and slide it into the centre of the deck. Make sure that you do not spread any of the cards at this point or someone may notice that the majority of the cards are face up and this would give away the secret of the trick.

The next bit of patter is important as it covers a secret move that you are going to make. Say 'I am going to find your card in less time than it takes you to blink. So watch carefully, I'm not even going to cheat by putting the cards behind my back like this'. This line will usually get a laugh because you are going to do exactly what you told them you were not going to do. Put both hands behind your back and turn over the top card of the pack, this action puts all the cards the same way up apart from the chosen card. It takes a split second and everyone will assume that it was just a joke as you obviously did not have time to do anything. Magicians are the only people in the world who are allowed to lie!

The trick is now done. All you have to do is spread the cards across the table and they will see one face up card in the pack – and it is their chosen card.

Above: Only spread the top half of the cards and there will be no chance of the audience seeing the face up card on the bottom of the deck.

Right: When replacing the card into the pack be careful not to spread the cards.

Left: Spread the cards on the table or between your hands to show the face up card – then take your well-deserved applause.

FIVE ACES

Everyone knows that there are only four aces so you may think that the title of this trick is misleading, you would be right. The five refers to a five of hearts (or any five) and the aces are the usual four. Now I have explained that I can get on with the trick! In this trick a card is selected and then found in an unusual way, but there is an extra climax to the trick that will knock the socks of any audience. A card is selected and placed back into the pack. On spreading the cards out the audience see a face up card – the five of hearts – not the chosen card, it seems that the trick has gone wrong. But you explain that this is a card which tells you where their card is. Count along the pack pushing out five cards and the fifth card is the correct card. Before the audience have a chance to respond you turn over the four cards that you pushed out and they are the four aces.

METHOD

Before you perform this trick you must stack the bottom of the deck in the following way. The bottom four cards are the four aces, above them you place a face up five (in this case I am using the five of hearts). You can do this by having the pack already set or run through the cards and quickly arrange them under the pretence of checking that they are all there.

Spread the top section of the cards between your hands as you did in the Upside-Down Card Mystery, remember that there is a face up card fifth from the bottom of the deck that the audience must not see. Have a card selected and remembered by the audience. While they are doing this place the pack on the table. To lose the card in the pack ask the spectator to place it on top of the deck and then cut the cards and complete the cut. The chosen card will then be somewhere in the middle of the deck and no-one knows where, which is true because at this

point you do not know where it is. You do know however that it is five cards below the face up card.

To find the card spread the cards across the table and point proudly at the face up card. Spectators are rarely backwards at coming forwards, they love to catch you out so someone will probably say 'that is not my card'. If they do, say 'I didn't say it

was!' This adds to the fun of the trick because someone has fallen into a trap. Say 'This is a card that tells me where your card is'. Count down five cards pushing the cards out of the spread as you go, turning over the fifth card will get you a round of applause, it is their card. Turning over the other four cards will get you a standing ovation as they are the four aces!

The set up on the bottom of the pack: four aces face down, the five of hearts (or any five) face up and the rest of the pack face down.

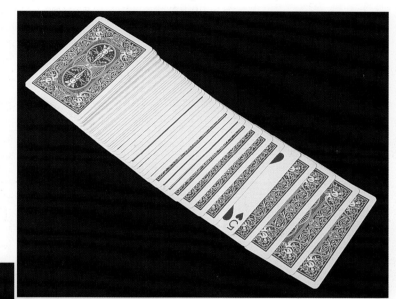

Left: As you count the cards below the five push them forward, turn the fifth card over – it is the chosen card.

Below: The other four cards are the four aces giving this trick a really strong climax.

15

KEY CARDS

There are many methods for finding a card that has been lost in the pack, my favourite is the key card. There are also many different types of key card tricks that can be done using the key card principle. Here is a trick that will explain how it works. A card is chosen and then lost in the pack, but the magician can find it in a number of ways.

METHOD

There is no need for any set up with this trick so you can freely shuffle the pack or let someone else shuffle it. Have a card selected by spreading the cards out between your two hands and asking someone to take a free sample.
Square up the deck while they look at and remember the card. It is always a good idea to have the card remembered by more than one person, it helps to keep everyone involved in the trick and eliminates the chance of someone forgetting the name of their card (believe me, this happens!)

The card must now be returned to and lost in the pack. To do this, hold the pack in your left hand and lift off about half of the cards with your right hand. Ask your helper to replace the card on top and hold out your left hand. As you do this take a sneaky look at the bottom card of the stock in your right hand. Remember this card as

it will be the 'key' to finding the chosen card. Place the cards in your right hand on top of the cards in your left, the chosen card is now underneath the key card. At this stage you can give the cards a brief overhand shuffle, the chance of separating the key card and the chosen card is only slight (do not do a riffle shuffle as that will almost definitely separate the cards).

To conclude the trick you must find the chosen card. Start dealing the cards on to the table face up, as you do this you are looking for the key card. Tell the helper to

Above: The key card is here marked with an X. Try and make your glance at the card as natural as possible.

Below: The chosen card (five of clubs) is directly above the key card (not marked in your act, of course).

watch the cards and to say nothing if he sees his card. When you spot the key you will find that the next card is the card that was selected. Instead of turning that card and saying 'here it is' you now have the chance to play an extra joke. Keep dealing past their card but mentally note which one it is. After an extra half a dozen cards have been dealt say that the next card you turn over will be their card. This will be met with some disbelief as they have seen you deal their card on the table – you could even offer a small wager. Whatever they say reach into the face up cards and turn over the card that you know to be theirs. It is a joke that always gets a good laugh as long as you are not serious about the wager!

AN ALTERNATIVE ENDING

Another way of bringing this trick to a climax is to turn the pack over and show the cards to your helper. What you say is that you want them to be sure that the card is lost in the pack. What you are doing is looking for the key card. When you find it look at the card that is above it, this will be the chosen card, in our example it is the five of clubs. Keep pushing cards across from your left hand spelling their card silently, one letter to one card as you push the cards across, the first letter (F) is the key card, the next is the 'I' and so on, until you reach the end of 'FIVE OF CLUBS'. Cut the cards at this point moving all the cards beneath to the top of the pack, turn the cards over and square them up. Ask them to name their card and when they do spell it out, one letter for each card, the next card will be their selection.

ADVANCED KEY CARD TECHNIQUES

The key card trick on the previous page is one of the basic tricks of magic and is known by many people. Most of them do not realize that there are other ways of using the same principle and they will easily be fooled if you change the handling slightly. In this version the cards are shuffled and you do not need to take that sneaky look at the key card.

SHUFFLING OFF A KEY CARD

The key card for this effect is the top card. You need to catch sight of it while shuffling the cards prior to performing the trick. Have a card selected as before and then cut the cards and proffer the bottom half of the pack for return of the card. When the card is returned there is no need to look at the bottom card of the top portion of deck. The key card we are going to use is the top card which is going to be placed in the correct position by shuffling.

The stock of cards in your right hand are turned into the position for an overhand shuffle (the key card in the picture is clearly marked with an X). To start the shuffle pull off a single (key) card first and then continue the shuffle until all the cards are gone from your right hand. This is a much more natural way of having the card put back in the deck and the audience will remember that the cards were shuffled after replacing the card, yet it is this action that is achieving the trick.

Follow the routines above with this handling of the key card principle and

Above: Shuffle the single key card on top of the chosen card...

Left: ...then continue shuffling until you run out of cards.

people will be really fooled. They will credit you with great skill and amazing ability in controlling cards when you are merely doing a slight variation of a trick that they probably know.

THE SHORT CORNER KEY CARD

This is another version of the key card technique but it is much more devious and will take a little practice to master. But first you will need to make a short corner key card. Take any playing card, for practising I suggest that you use a joker, and remove a couple of millimetres from two diagonally opposite corners that have been marked (as in the illustration). A pair of scissors will do this but nail clippers could have been designed specifically for making this gimmicked card, they cut cleanly and because of the shape put a neat curved corner on the card.

If you riffle your thumb down the outside corner of the cards you will notice a definite click as the short corner goes past. This is because two cards (the card above and the short card) pass as one, the double thickness will be audible to you as you know what to listen for, but the audience will not notice it. As well as the noise there is a 'feel' to the short corner, with a little practice you will be able to riffle down the cards once to locate approximately where it is, and then riffle again and stop at exactly the right place. There is no right or wrong technique for doing this, play with it for a while and it will just click into place. If you cannot find the key card it is probably right at the top or right at the bottom of the pack, simply cut the cards and try again. When you have located the short card, cut the pack at this point and the short corner will be at the bottom. If the chosen card was below the short corner card it will now be on the top of the deck.

Above: By shortening opposite corners of the card it will not matter which way round the pack is, you will still find the key card.

Left: Riffle down the corner of the cards with your thumb and you will hear and feel the short corner card.

SOME MORE WAYS OF USING KEY CARDS

1. Start with the short corner card on top of the pack. Let the spectator cut the pack and take any card from the bottom stock, look at it, place it on the top stock and complete the cut. The deck can be cut as often as you like and the key and chosen cards will stay together. The chosen card will always be on top of the key card. If you start the sequence with the key card on the bottom then the chosen card will be underneath the key card.

2. With the key card either on the top or the bottom, hand the whole pack to a spectator. Ask him or her, while your back is turned, to remove a card from the centre of the deck, look at it, replace it on the top and give the pack as many cuts as he would like. If the key card starts on top the chosen card will be on top of the key card. If it starts on the bottom then the chosen card will be underneath it.

3. With the key card on the bottom, give the cards to a spectator to deal any number of cards onto the table. Tell them to look at the card where they stopped and when they have remembered it, to drop the rest of the pack on top. The selected card will be directly beneath the key card.

NOTE : When using key cards the pack can be cut as many times as you like without fear of separating the key from the chosen card. The only time they could be separated is when the key is cut to the top and the chosen card was above the key card. If this happens then the chosen card will now be on the bottom of the pack. The reverse is true if the chosen card is underneath the key card.

CUTTING THE ACES

To prove your skill as a card sharp you need to learn how to cut the aces. This takes a great deal of practice and is beyond the scope of a beginner. In this trick you get the spectator to cut the aces and they will have no idea how they did it.

METHOD

To start the trick have all four aces on top of the deck. If you are using this trick as a follow up to the Five Aces trick then simply pick up the aces and drop them on the top of the pack and you will be all set for Cutting The Aces.

The first step is to ask someone to cut the pack into four piles. While this is being done, keep a careful eye on the section that has the four aces on top. The spectator is now going to mix around the top cards in the following way. Ask them to pick up the first pile of cards (not the one with the aces on top), place three cards from the top to the bottom, then one card on each of the other three piles. This is repeated for the other three piles but you must make sure that the ace pile is the last.

The above procedure will put three extra cards on top of the aces so when the ace pile is picked up the three extra cards are the ones that are put on the bottom and then the aces are placed on top of each pile. Ask the spectator if they know what they have just done, when they say no show them that they have cut the aces by turning the top card of each pile. A nice line to finish with is 'well if you can do that I'm not playing cards with you!'

Above: The cards are cut into four piles and you must indicate which pile they are to pick up first.

Right: The spectator will be very surprised to find that he has cut to the four aces, and he will have no idea how it was done.

THE STACKED DECK

A stack is a magician's term meaning a group of cards in a pre-arranged order. A stacked deck is a whole pack that is set up so that you can tell what the next card is by looking at the one before. The easiest stack would be to have the cards in suit order, ace to king of clubs followed by ace to king of hearts etc. This would be very easy to use but because the order is obvious you could not show the faces of the cards to the audience. The most popular stack used today is the Si Stebbins Stack. There are two things to remember in this stack: firstly, the suits run in order clubs, hearts, spades, diamonds. This can be easily remembered by using the mnemonic CHaSeD; secondly, the cards increase in value in steps of three (i.e. ace, four, seven, etc.): jacks, queens, and kings are valued at eleven, twelve and thirteen respectively. When you get to thirteen (king) start counting at the ace again so the card after a king is a three, after a queen a two and after a jack you have the ace. When the cards are laid out as in the illustration the order is very clear but if you pass the cards from hand to hand and take a casual glance then it will look like a shuffled deck.

Arrange a pack of cards in the correct sequence and play with it until you get the hang of the system. Practise by testing yourself, call out the names of the cards as you turn them over, learn to work out which card is above and which card is below the card you are looking at. Another thing worth noting about this stack is that every thirteenth card has a similar value and every fourth card has a similar suit.

Do not shuffle the pack or you will upset the stack, you can however cut the cards as often as you like and the stack will not be spoiled. The top card will always be the next in the sequence after the bottom card, and as long as each cut is completed then the sequence will not be broken. When you have reached a level of competence with the stack try some of the tricks on the next page.

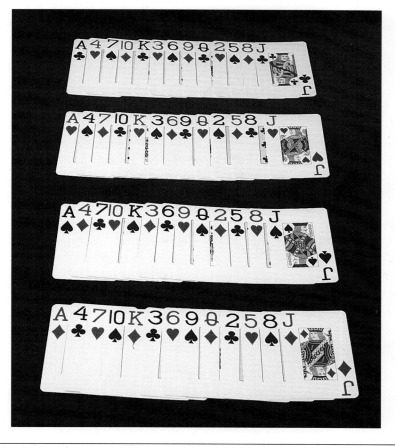

The Si Stebbins Stack. Cards increase in increments of three and run clubs, hearts, spades, diamonds.

TRICKS WITH A STACKED DECK

MIND READING REVELATION

Using a deck of cards that is stacked in the Si Stebbins method it is easy to show your 'powers' as a mind reader. To start with, you must cut the cards several times and then show the cards to the audience so they know the cards aren't all the same. Then fan the cards face downwards between your hands and invite a spectator to remove and look at a card of their choice. Casually take all the cards above the card that was selected and place them underneath the rest of the pack and square them up. As you do this you should have no problem glancing at the bottom card. To determine the value of the chosen card you must add three to the glimpsed card and then work out the suit using the mnemonic CHaSeD. If the card on the bottom of the pack was the three of diamonds then the card that was chosen would be the six of clubs.

Do not reveal the name of the card immediately, instead pretend that you are reading the spectator's mind. Ask them to concentrate on the card and then gradually reveal the cards by saying things like 'I think you have a black card, yes?... It's a spade and it's a spot card, no that's wrong... it's a club, but it's definitely a spot card, imagine the pattern of the spots for me, imagine them on a cinema screen... I see six spots, your card was the six of clubs, am I correct?'

Ask the spectator to show the chosen card to the audience, proving that your experiment in telepathy was successful. Take the card and drop it on top of the pack and the stack has automatically reset itself, no need to re-order the cards you are ready to go on to the next effect.

MULTIPLE REVELATION

As a follow up to the previous effect you could try the multiple revelation. This effect seems much harder to do as a number of cards are chosen. But using a stacked deck it is just as easy to name ten chosen cards as it is to name one.

Ask a volunteer to cut the pack and remove about ten cards at that point. He or she keeps the top card and then mixes and hands out the other cards to other spectators (this is a great trick because it involves a large number of people). As you retrieve the rest of the pack, complete the cut and make a mental note of the bottom card. You know from the identity of the bottom card which cards come next, so ask the spectators to concentrate on their cards. When you call out the name of their card they must hand it back to you. This not only verifies the fact that you are correct, it also means that you put the cards back in the correct order so the Si Stebbins Stack is retained for future use.

If you slowly reveal the nature of the card (ie. 'I'm getting the image of a black card and I think it's a picture card...') you will often find that someone in the audience reacts when you start hinting at their card. Use this to your advantage by pointing them out and saying 'I'm getting

a very clear image coming from you sir, is the card you are holding the king of spades?' This adds to the effect as you are now divining who has the cards as well as what the cards are.

THE REVERSED CARD

Ask a spectator to put the deck of cards behind his back, he is to cut the cards and complete the cut as many times as he wants to. When he is satisfied that no-one knows the whereabouts of any card he is to take the top card, turn it over and push it into the middle of the pack. The simple action of retrieving the pack will give you a chance to glimpse the bottom card which will tell you the name of the card that the spectator reversed in the pack. Because of this you know which card was reversed in the pack without touching the cards or looking through the pack, even the volunteer has no way of knowing which card was reversed.

Below: A stacked deck makes it easy to find a lost card. If a card is chosen and replaced in the wrong place it stands out because the sequence of clubs, hearts, spades, diamonds (CHaSeD) is broken. The eight of diamonds is out of place and must have been the chosen card.

THE ONE AHEAD PRINCIPLE

This is a principle that has many applications for the magician or the mind reader. To explain how it works the first trick is a card trick where the pack is cut into three random piles yet you can divine the names of the top cards of the piles.

METHOD

Before starting this trick you need to know the name of the top card. It is a simple matter to glimpse it while shuffling or simply look at the bottom card and move it to the top of the pack, for our example we will say the top card is the three of diamonds. Having done this you are ready to start.

Place the cards on the table and ask the spectator to cut the cards into three piles, they don't have to be even, any number of cards per pile is fine. While this is being done you must keep an eye on the position of the top card, in the illustrations it is clearly marked with an 'X'.

Tell the spectator that you are going to name the three cards that he cut to. You only know the name of one card at the moment, the card that was on the top of the deck. Point to a pile, not the pile with the known card, and say 'this card is the three of diamonds', it's not, but the spectator does not know this so it doesn't matter. Pick up the card and look at it (don't let the spectator see it), smile to yourself as if you were correct, and remember its name, for example, the five of hearts.

Point to another pile, again not the pile with the known card, and say 'this card is the five of hearts', follow the same procedure as before. Pick it up, look at it, remember its name (e.g. its the king of clubs). Now point to the last pile. The top card is the three of diamonds but you call it by the name of the card that you just picked up, the king of clubs.

At this stage you have picked up three cards and named them. The names you called out are the names of the three cards, you just changed the order but you have the right three cards in your hand. All you need to do is prove to the spectator that you are correct, so lay down the three cards face up calling out their names as you do.

The one ahead principle is just as it says, each time you pick up a card you know what to call the next card, and by knowing the name of the last card you stay one ahead of yourself throughout the trick.

Left: When the cards are cut into three piles remember the position of the top (known) card and pick this pile last.

Below: The last card that you pick up is the card you named first, but you call it by the name of the previous card. Result – three correctly named cards!

Above: After naming the card, pick it up and look at it. Acknowledge to yourself that you are correct and get ready for the next card.

MESSAGE READING

This is another use of the one ahead principle. Ask a number of people to write a few words on a piece of paper and then to fold the papers in half. You are going to divine what is written on the papers and to do this you need to know the words on one paper to start it off. The easiest way to achieve this is to tell a friend to write a particular message on his paper (magicians

call this 'using a stooge'). When collecting the papers make sure that the known message is on the bottom of the pile.

You are now going to divine the words or messages on the papers. Pick up the top paper and hold it to your forehead. You now tell everyone the contents of the message, only it is the pre-arranged message that you announce. Open the paper, pretend to check you are correct

and memorize the actual words written down. These are to be read out as the contents of the next paper. Proceed with the same pattern until every message has been read out and ask the people to verify that each message was correct. Don't be tempted to go on too long with this, half a dozen messages are more than enough!

CARD FORCING

You can force rhubarb, and force open a door, but what is forcing a card? This is a term used by magicians that means you are seemingly giving a totally free choice but in reality the card selected is the one that the magician wants you to choose. You are forcing the spectator to take a particular card. The easiest way to force a card is to offer a choice from a pack of cards that are all the same, but you will not be able to do any other tricks with the pack! Here are a couple of methods that will enable you to force a card using a normal pack.

THE TURN OVER FORCE

The force card is the top card which you have already memorized (we have marked it with a cross so that you can keep track of it in the example). This can be done on the table or in the hands depending on the situation. As a rule I prefer to get someone to do it in their hands as it gives the impression of a freer choice.

Give the cards to the spectator to hold and ask them to cut off about one third of the cards, turn them over and put them back on the top of the deck. This is repeated, but this time they are to cut two thirds of the cards, turn them over and drop them on top of the deck.

Take back the cards and spread them across the table. Ask the spectator to slide out the first face-down card (this will be the card that was the top card at the start of the force). Before they take the card you can emphasize the freedom of their choice by saying 'You cut the cards twice and I

didn't make you do it in any particular place, is that correct?' They will answer positively but the truth is you have forced this choice on them.

Left: Ask the helper to turn over one third of the cards.

Below: Next, turn over about two thirds of the cards, make sure the second cut is beneath the first cut.

Below: Spread the cards on the table and slide out the first face-down card.

THE CROSS CUT FORCE

The card you are about to force should be on the top of the pack and the cards should be on the table. Ask a spectator to cut off about half of the cards and to place them beside the rest of the pack. As soon as this is done pick up the bottom half of the cards and drop them on top of the top half of the cards to make a cross. You must emphasize at this point the freedom of choice that the spectator had, they could have cut anywhere but they chose this particular point. When they have agreed with the freedom of choice pick up the top portion of the 'cross' and casually throw the next card on the table, ask them to look at the card that they cut to. As this happens you can square up the deck and be confident in the knowledge that you have successfully forced a card.

The force card looks as if it has come from the middle of the pack when only a few moments ago it was on the top.

STOP

This is another favourite trick of mine, simple to do and very impressive. The cards can be shuffled by a spectator who then deals a pile onto the table until they decide to stop. You drop your wallet on top of the cards and ask the spectator to look inside. They open the wallet to find a piece of paper with the words 'You will stop at the two of clubs'. Sure enough, when the last card dealt onto the table is turned over it is the two of clubs!

PREPARATION

You will need a wallet containing a message that says 'YOU WILL STOP AT THE TWO OF CLUBS' and you must take the two of clubs out of the pack. The card and wallet are put in your pocket next to each other, practise removing them from your pocket at the same time without flashing the card.

METHOD

By now you will have probably worked this out for yourself! Ask the spectator to shuffle the cards and then deal a pile onto the table, it does not matter how many cards but the more the merrier in this trick. While this is happening reach into your pocket and get the wallet/card out. As soon as the spectator stops dealing, drop your wallet and the card on top of the pile of cards that are on the table. The trick is now done, from here you can concentrate on the presentation. Re-affirm the fact that the spectator shuffled the cards, that he dealt as many cards as he wanted and stopped when it suited him. Ask him to open the wallet and read the message. Pick up the wallet and turn over the top card to show that you are correct.

Above: **2.** As soon as the spectator stops dealing drop the wallet on the cards.

Right: **3.** Open the wallet to reveal the message.

Above: **1.** While the cards are dealt on the table get the wallet/card ready. Do not flash the card to the spectators.

Right: **4.** Let the spectator turn the card and take your applause.

THREE-AND-A-HALF OF CLUBS

At the start of the trick you place a prediction card face down on the table. You say that the prediction card will be the same suit as the chosen card and half the value, so if the chosen card was a 10 of diamonds the prediction will be the 5 of diamonds. A card is chosen but it seems that an error has crept in, the chosen card is the seven of clubs which means your prediction should be the three-and-a-half of clubs! You turn over your prediction to show that it is correct.

METHOD

You will need to make a special three-and-a-half card. You can do this by cutting up another card or using rub down lettering. This is your prediction card and is simply

placed face down on the table at the start of the trick. You then need to force the seven of clubs using one of the methods on page 22, and get ready for a big laugh at the climax of the trick.

OUT OF CARDS

This is an unusual trick which gets away from the 'pick a card' idea and has a nice surprise climax. The spectator is asked to cut a number of cards from the top of the deck and put them behind his or her back. As this is done you should avert your gaze so you will have no idea how many cards have been taken. You then take a number of cards and take it in turns with the spectator to put cards on the table. The spectator deals down his last card and your next card has a message written on it that says 'YOU HAVE JUST RUN OUT OF CARDS'.

PREPARATION
You will need to make the special card. To do this you can write or type the message on a piece of white paper and then glue it onto the face of a joker. If you have access to a computer then you can print it with large bold type and it will look very professional. This card is positioned as the twenty-first card in the deck.

METHOD
Ask your spectator to cut off a number of cards from the top of the deck. The only thing you need to make sure of is that they take less than twenty-one cards. To do this just say 'don't take too many cards or we'll be here all night, between ten and twenty would be a good number'. When he has done this get him to put the cards behind his back or in his pocket so you can't see them.

It is now up to you to take some cards. You must take twenty-one cards and at the same time you must reverse the order. To do this deal the cards onto the table and count silently to yourself until you have the right number of cards. When you have a pile of twenty-one cards on the table put the remainder of the pack aside and pick up the twenty-one cards.

The cards are now to be dealt onto the

SIMPLETON'S STACK

This is a simple method of stacking a deck that will help you find a chosen card. Take all the twos, threes, fives, sixes, nines, jacks and queens and mix them together. Put them underneath the rest of the cards. If you spread through the cards they will look as if the order is random. All the cards listed above are easily remembered and identified as they all have a hook, for instance the curly part of the 5 or the bottom of the J. Any card selected from the top of the pack will not have a hook. Have one of those cards selected by spreading the top half of the cards and make sure it is returned to the bottom half and you will find the chosen card easily, it will be the only hookless card amongst the hooks.

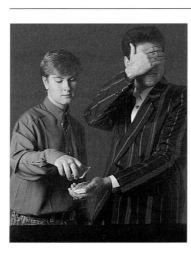

Left: It does not matter how many cards are taken as long as it is less than twenty-one.

Right: Deal twenty-one cards onto the table to reverse the order of the cards.

Below: Your prepared card will automatically be on top of your pack as the spectator runs out of cards.

table alternately. You must deal the first card, then the spectator, then you and so on. The spectator will run out of cards just before the prepared card is dealt onto the table. This is a mathematical trick and it works because as you reverse the order of the twenty-one cards you put the prepared card in the correct place for the climax of the trick – regardless of how many cards were taken.

DINNER TABLE MAGIC

One of the best places to perform magic is at a table after dinner. The atmosphere is relaxed and people are usually in the right mood to sit back and enjoy a couple of tricks. There are many tricks in this book that lend themselves to the after-dinner environment. In fact any tricks that can be performed without too much moving around are suitable. Card tricks, money tricks, rope tricks, any tricks that are good fun and entertaining are ideal. In this chapter you will find a few tricks that are designed for use at the dinner table. Most of them use props that will already be on the table, so at any meal, after the food has disappeared, you will be ready to dish up some diverse deceptions to enthral and entertain.

WHERE DID THE SALT POT GO

This is without doubt one of my favourite tricks. It is very strong from a magical point of view and yet it is still easy to do. When you read the directions you may think that you will not get away with it – but try it once and you will realize how good this trick is. A coin is placed on the table and while explaining that the coin is going to pass through the table you wrap a salt pot up in a serviette (napkin). The coin is tapped three times with the salt pot but it does not want to pass through the table. Then all of a sudden, you smash your hand down on the salt pot and it vanishes. With your other hand you reach under the table and produce the salt pot. It seems that the coin did not want to go so the salt pot went in its place.

METHOD

This trick employs a technique that magicians call lapping. At the right time, which is when the attention of the audience is somewhere else, the salt pot is dropped into the lap. The serviette holds the shape of the salt pot so the audience think that they can 'see' the salt pot right up to the moment it is slapped through the table. Follow the moves carefully and you will have a lot of success with this trick. Don't try this trick when you are standing up because your lap won't be there and you will just drop salt all over the floor!

PERFORMANCE

The first stage is to borrow a coin and place it on the table as you explain that the coin is going to pass through the solid wooden table. While you are talking you also wrap up the salt pot in a serviette. It is important that you wrap the serviette tightly around the salt pot because you want the serviette to retain the shape of the pot when you drop it into your lap in a few moments. Don't tear a paper serviette, just pull it tight and it will hold the necessary shape. Tap the coin three times with the salt pot, this is done for two reasons, firstly to emphasize the fact that the solid pot is

wrapped in the serviette and secondly to focus attention on the coin.

As you tap the pot on the coin tell the audience to watch the coin very closely as in a couple of seconds it is going to pass through the table. You are now about to lap the salt pot so the timing of the next few moves are important. After tapping the coin with the wrapped salt pot held in your right hand you move the right hand back to a position so the salt pot is over your lap and past the edge of the table. At the same time your left hand draws attention to the coin on the table as you point out that the coin is still on top of the table. When the pot has cleared the table edge, gently release the pressure of your grip and it will fall into your lap. This move takes a split second and will not be noticed by anyone. They have been told that the magic is going to happen to the coin, they will not be bothered about the salt pot, so you have plenty of time to lap it. The move must be smooth as any jerky or rushed movement will draw attention to the salt pot/serviette in your right hand.

After you have lapped the salt pot the serviette will retain the pot shape. But do not squeeze, your grip on the serviette must be very light or it will lose its shape and give the game away. Place the serviette over the coin and as you say 'watch this' slap your hand loudly on the table. The bang of your hand will make people jump, adding a surprise element to the trick. Then you immediately tell them that the coin has stayed put but the salt pot seems to have passed through the solid table. Reach under the table with your left hand and pretend to pick the salt pot from the centre of the underside of the table. All you really do is pick it up from your lap.

The trick is very effective from most viewpoints and with a little experience it can be performed with people all around you. Anyone sitting to one side of you may catch a glimpse of the pot as it is dropped into your lap. To avoid this you must draw their attention to the coin on the table as you lap the pot. Do this by looking at

Left: As the salt pot is wrapped up tightly in the serviette try to match as much of the shape as possible, this helps to keep the illusion that the pot is still there.

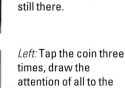

Left: Tap the coin three times, draw the attention of all to the coin.

Below: The moment the salt pot is lapped. Note the left hand 'pointing' to the coin while the salt pot is discreetly dropped in the lap.

Left: Make as much noise as you can when you 'slap' the salt pot through the table. Use the element of surprise.

Below: Reach under the table as you say 'I'm sorry, the salt pot went through the table instead of the coin – I can never get this trick right!'

them directly before you do the lapping move, tell them to watch the coin very closely, after all, they are the nearest so they must make sure you do not cheat. After telling them this and giving them good reason for watching the coin they will ignore the movement of your other hand with the salt pot/serviette.

This trick is just as effective with a mixer bottle or a small vase so you can do it even if someone has pinched the cruet.

FORK BENDING

Do not read this trick expecting to become the next Uri Geller. This is not so much a magic trick as a dinner table stunt which is a lot of fun to do. My favourite place to perform this is in a restaurant. Just as the waiter is walking up to take your order, this is what he sees : One of his customers picks up a fork and without a care in the world bends it in half. As he approaches the table he will be about to ask what they think they are playing at (or he might be about to throw them out!) But as he arrives the customer looks up and the waiter is stunned to see that the fork is not really bent at all. I have ended up teaching this trick to many waiters as they can't wait to wind up the other staff by showing it to them.

Another great place to do this is when your mother-in-law has laid the table with her best silver knives and forks for an important dinner party – but be ready to run afterwards – she may not find it that funny! One of the best things about being a magician is that you learn all sorts of practical jokes for any and every occasion; this is one of the best.

METHOD

The fork is held in two hands as in the first picture. To give the illusion that the fork is really bending you must act as if you are exerting great pressure, a little shaking of the hands, and push down and forward with your hands. From the front view it will look as if you have just bent the fork at an angle of 90°. From the side view you can see what really happens. As the hands push downwards the handle is allowed to slip back through your fingers so the fork does not really bend. The handle of the fork is only held by the little finger of the

right hand which acts as a pivot point. The whole movement is covered from sight from all angles apart from your immediate left. Anyone sitting there will see what is happening, but don't worry, they are unlikely to say anything when they notice the shocked faces of the other people at the table.

When the shock of your audience has reached a peak put the fork back on the table and let them see that it is not really bent – if they don't laugh be ready to hide! Do not delay too long before revealing the fork is OK. You must not give the audience time to look away or they will miss the joke.

I have had a lot of fun with this stunt, the funniest moment was when a friend of mine, having seen me 'bend' the fork said 'That's easy, anyone can do that' and before I could stop him he picked up a fork and bent it in half – that day we did get thrown out of the restaurant!

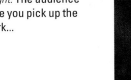
Right: The audience see you pick up the fork...

Below:...and bend it to an angle of 90°.

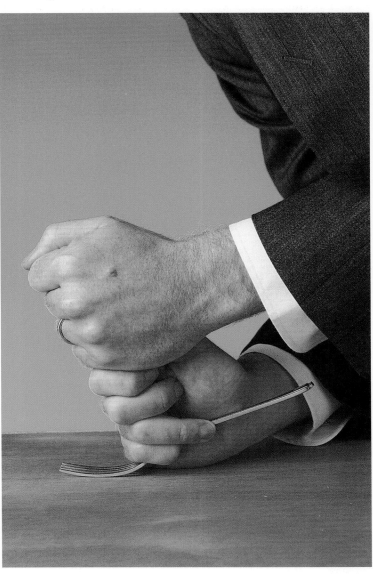

Right: Viewed from the side you can see that the fork is not really bent at all.

COIN FROM BREAD ROLL

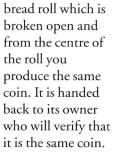

A coin is borrowed and, if you like, it can be marked for later identification. With a little bit of help from some magic salt the coin has vanished. Someone passes you a bread roll which is broken open and from the centre of the roll you produce the same coin. It is handed back to its owner who will verify that it is the same coin.

METHOD

There are two parts to this trick, firstly making the coin disappear, and secondly, making it appear from the bread roll. To vanish the coin you must learn the French Drop, described on page 60. There is a slight modification to the move that makes the handling a little easier. After the French Drop, the coin is retained in the fingers of the left hand but the audience think that you have placed the coin into your right hand. At this point your left hand (containing the concealed coin in the finger palm position) picks up the salt pot and shakes some 'magic salt' on the hand that the audience thinks contains the coin. By doing this the spectators will be convinced the coin is in the right hand. (If you have got a salt pot in your left hand the coin can't be there). This is the same reason magicians use a magic wand, to hide the fact that there is something else hidden in their hand. If there is no salt pot you could use a chopstick or a pencil as a magic wand. After the vanish the coin will be secretly retained in your left fingers.

You are now going to reproduce the coin from the bread roll. It is always best to use someone else's roll. They may accuse you of fiddling with your own roll but to use another avoids any suspicion of foul play. Take the roll in your right hand and place it into your left hand on top of the coin (see fig 1). The coin will be completely hidden by the roll so there is no need to worry about being found out

Above: 1. Viewed from underneath, the starting position for loading the coin into the roll.

Above: 3. As you feel the break open up, push the coin into the centre of the roll.

at this stage. You are now going to break the roll in half and push the coin into the roll in one smooth action. Firstly, you need to break the crust on the underside of the roll. This is achieved by gripping the roll on the sides, pushing down with your thumbs and pulling up with your fingers (see fig 2). As soon as you feel the crust underneath break the coin is pushed into the centre of the roll (fig 3), you then reverse the pressure and start to break the roll from the top, using your thumbs to break open the roll (fig 4). As you do this final break the roll should be tilted towards the audience and the coin can be produced from the middle of the roll. Let the spectator remove the coin without your even having touched it. Have the coin checked by its owner and you have performed a miracle.

Above: 2. Pull up with your fingers and the underside of the roll will begin to break open.

Right: 4. The coin is produced from the centre of the roll – it must have been cooked in there!

THE BOUNCING BREAD ROLL

I never knew bread rolls could be so much fun! This is a quickie that will always raise a laugh. As you sit around the table, pick up a bread roll and get excited as you tell the assembled people that this is a new type of bread roll that you have read about in the paper. It has all the nutritional value of a normal bread roll and some rather unusual properties. 'Watch this', you exclaim, and then you proceed to throw the roll to the floor and it bounces straight back up again! Don't forget to watch the faces of the people watching, and it's even more fun if they try to bounce their bread rolls – it won't work for them – unless like you they have got a copy of this book.

METHOD

This trick sounds very simple but you will have to practise the timing to perfect it. Although it will look and sound as if the roll has bounced off the floor, what has actually happened is your hand has taken the bread roll out of sight below the line of the table and then thrown it back up again. There are three parts to the effect. Firstly, you hold the roll in either hand and make a downwards throwing action. The completion of the throw is below the line of the table so no-one sees you keeping hold of the roll. Your eyes follow the roll's imaginary journey to the floor. Secondly, as you imagine the roll hitting the floor, you tap your foot on the ground to create the sound of the bounce. Out of context the sound is unconvincing but if you get the timing right no-one will give the fake sound a second thought. Finally, as your eyes follow the imaginary journey of the roll bouncing up, you gently flick your wrist and throw the roll up into the air. This last move is again hidden by the table. The timing is important on this move and must be practised to perfection.

HOW TO PRACTISE

The easiest way to learn this move is to use a tennis ball. With the ball in your right hand throw it to the floor, watch it go down and try and tap your foot at the same time as it hits the floor. After about ten throws you will find this quite easy. Now forget about the foot for a moment and practise flicking the ball back up from below the table line. When you have mastered this so that the ball flies straight up, go on to the next stage, pretending to throw the ball down and flicking it back up again. When you have managed to get the timing right on these two moves you can put it all together and practise the throw, tap, flick sequence until you have perfected the timing.

Right: Throw the bread roll down, remember to look at where it should be, not where it is.

Below: Follow the flight of the roll back up into the air. If you believe it then the audience will.

29

THE ZOMBIE ROLL

You will have probably seen the trick where a magician covers a silver ball with a cloth, and then looks on with amazement as the ball floats up and dances on top of the cloth. As with so many tricks, finding out how they are done can be disappointing. This is an impromptu version of that trick, the method is virtually the same only instead of a silver ball we are using a bread roll, and instead

Right: Always watch the roll as it floats and keep the hands as far apart as the napkin allows. Do not let the centre of the napkin sag or the fork may come into view.

Below: Show surprise when the roll begins to float. With a little acting you will convince people that the roll is actually tugging at the napkin.

of a fancy silk cloth we are using a napkin. The traditional floating zombie ball uses a wire gimmick that runs from the ball to the magician's hand and it is this that raises and 'floats' the ball. For the zombie roll the gimmick we are going to use is the fork.

METHOD

While the attention of everyone on the table is directed to someone else, pick up a fork and stick it into the side of a bread roll. Do not worry about being seen as most people will also be buttering or breaking open their rolls. At the same time, your action, although slightly different, will fit in with what everyone

else is doing. The roll and fork can be left on your plate in full view while you pick up the napkin and get ready to start the trick.

Draw attention back to yourself by announcing that you are going to amaze them with your magical powers. When they are all watching, show both sides of the napkin, holding it away from your body, with the fork and bread roll on the table between the napkin and your body. The bread roll will remain hidden behind the flourish with the napkin so the

fact that it has a fork stuck in the side of it will still not be noticed. Lower the napkin so that it covers the roll and the fork, one of the top corners should land on the end of the fork handle. Pick up the fork and napkin with your fingers and lift the roll up. The napkin will rise with the roll in the centre – spooky stuff. With a little mime work you can pretend that the roll is pulling you and has taken on a life all of its own. The roll then starts to calm down and gently bobs on the top edge of the napkin.

To end the trick you can do the following. Make the roll float about a bit and just when you seem to have it under control make it duck down behind the napkin and completely disappear. This is done by lowering the napkin so the bottom edge is on the table and then dropping the fork and roll into your lap (make sure that the fork does not hit the table or miss your lap and land on the floor). As soon as the roll is out of sight, raise the napkin back up a little and watch the place where the roll is meant to be hovering (just out of sight behind the napkin). On the count of three you can screw the napkin into a tight ball and the roll will have vanished.

Don't give away the secret. It may be funny at the time but remember that most people lose interest in magic once they know how it is done.

30

THE LEVITATING PAPER

Plan A viewed from above.

The first part of this trick is a well known gag but the follow up is impressive enough to blow people's socks off. You can perform it with a paper, a menu, a place mat or any similar-shaped object. To start with you show the audience what they will consider to be a very old schoolboy joke where the paper seems to stick to your hand. A few moments later you do the same trick only this time they will be totally fooled.

PLAN A

This is a simple trick which most people remember learning at school. The paper is held against the palm of your left hand by the first finger of your right hand. The other fingers of that hand are gripping your left wrist. This is made very clear in the picture. If someone in the audience does not know this old trick then they will be quite impressed at this stage but someone is bound to know how it is done and take delight in giving the game away. This is when you revert to plan B.

Below: Plan A viewed from below.

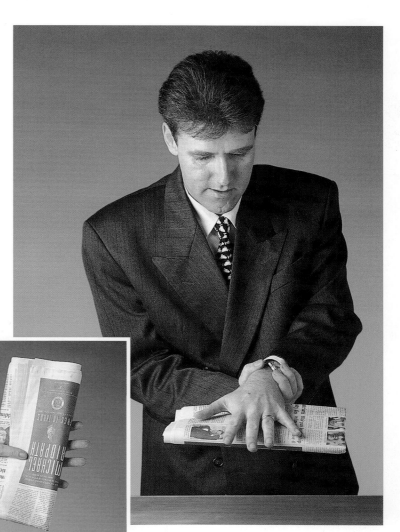

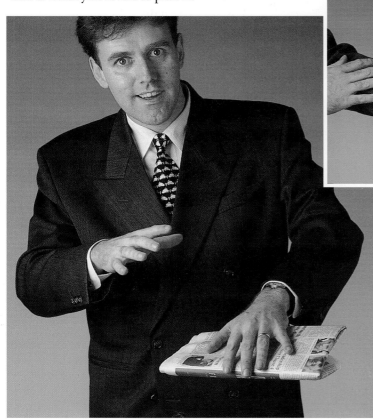

Above: If you are performing this and a knife is not to hand then try a chopstick, a pencil, a ruler...

Left: Be prepared for a very surprised audience when you remove your right hand and show the paper still levitating.

PLAN B

This is the second stage of the trick. The effect is very similar in that a paper sticks to your hand. Your movements will be identical to the previous method only this time you can remove your right hand completely! The sight of the paper sticking to your hand is quite weird. The second levitation is achieved by secretly sliding a table knife under your watch strap. When it comes to doing the second levitation, all you need to do is slip the paper between your hand and the blade of the knife. Keep your right hand in the position that you used in plan A until you are accused of cheating again and then you can remove it to show the paper levitating all by itself.

31

VANISHING GLASS

An empty glass is covered with a handkerchief and then the glass and hanky together are lifted off the table. The magician throws the hanky into the air and the glass has vanished from sight.

METHOD

To make the glass vanish you will need to make a special fake handkerchief. It consists of two identical hankies, onto one of which you stick a circle of card or thin plastic that is approximately the same size as the

mouth of the glass that you intend to make vanish. If you intend to perform this trick a lot you should make the disc out of plastic; you can then wash the hanky without fear of the fake disintegrating. You will find that most glasses are of a similar size and it will be easy to find a glass of the right size if you are at a party or a restaurant (getting the glass to match the hanky saves making ten different sized fake hankies). When the plastic disc has been glued into position, sew the other hanky on top so that the plastic circle is hidden between the two. If you hold the plastic disc through the material of the hankerchief it will give the illusion of a glass or cup being held underneath. This illusion is part of the secret of the vanishing glass. To complete the illusion you will need to follow the performance details below.

PERFORMANCE

The performance of this trick requires a little practice but should be easily mastered. Firstly, you must cover the glass with the special hanky so that the plastic disc inside comes to rest on top of the glass. Now pick up the glass and the plastic disc together, the hanky should surround the glass but the form of the glass will be visible in the hanky. As you lift the glass

clear of the table, pull it back so that it is now clear of the edge of the table. At this point you let the glass slip out of your fingers but retain your grip on the plastic disc. The glass is either dropped into your lap if you are seated or caught in your left hand below the edge of the table if you are standing (this is shown in the pictures). The audience will be convinced that the glass is still under the cover because they can see its shape. All you have to do now is say a magic word and throw the hanky into the air. It will flutter lightly down and the glass has vanished.

Above: To make the fake hanky use a patterned material. White hankies tend to be a bit see-through and are therefore unsuitable.

Below: The outline and shape of the glass can be seen under the hanky. Make sure you get a firm grip on both the plastic disc and the glass and lift them up together.

If you have the courage you could try the following presentation. It is really cheeky and I have often used it. To do this you need the table to be littered with a number of glasses which are all close together. Cover one of them up with the fake hanky and lift the disc leaving the glass with the others on the table. As you lift the hanky make sure your eyes follow it and the spectators will also watch the hanky and assume you have picked up the glass because they can see the shape of it through the hanky. To make the glass vanish, just shake out the hanky. This method relies on bare-faced cheek but works really well in a bar when there are normally a number of empties on the table. Be brave and give it a try, you will have lots of fun with it.

Left: By covering the glass this way it is easy to place the plastic disc directly on top of the glass.

Below: To drop the glass release the grip slightly and let it slip through your fingers, keeping hold of the plastic disc. Make sure that your other hand is ready to catch the glass or, if seated, drop it into your lap.

THE KNIFE AND NAPKIN

A knife and three small pieces torn from a paper napkin are used in this little mystery. Both sides of the knife are shown and the audience is told about the strange things that happen when a reflective surface is combined with a sharp blade. Polish up the knife with the rest of the napkin and then lick and stick one of the small pieces of napkin onto the blade. You then turn the knife over and it seems that another piece has appeared on the reverse side of the blade. This is repeated with the second and third pieces of napkin. You only stuck on three pieces yet there are now six pieces of napkin on the knife. Three pieces are removed from one side of the blade and the three on the other side disappear. Then with a snap of your fingers there are six pieces of napkin back on the blade, three on each side.

METHOD

This is a trick that uses a move called the Paddle Move (see page 44). It is a simple sleight of hand move which gives the illusion that you are showing both sides of the knife blade when you are really showing the same side twice. This trick also requires a little preparation that should be done out of the sight of the audience. You need a knife and six little pieces of napkin or tissue. Three of the pieces are stuck onto the knife using a little dab of water from your water glass. The other three pieces are set aside for later use.

PERFORMANCE

The sequence of moves that you do can be varied depending on how you want to present the trick. This is the sequence of moves that I use when performing this trick after a dinner.

1. Lay the three pieces of napkin on the table and show both sides of the knife using the Paddle Move (the three pieces on the back of the blade will remain out of sight and the blade will look bare).
2. Pick up a piece of napkin and dab it on your tongue and stick it to the knife. Do the paddle move to show that another piece of napkin has appeared on the other side of the knife.

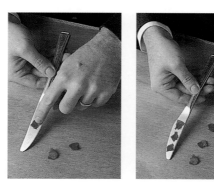

Carefully lick each piece and stick it on the blade. Keep your eyes open in case a piece starts to come loose, it may need more moisture to hold it in place.

Make sure the napkin pieces do not protrude over the edge of the blade of the knife. Practise the Paddle Move to make the pieces appear and disappear.

3. Repeat stage 2 with the second piece of napkin.
4. Stick the last piece of napkin on the knife blade and show that there are now three pieces on each side of the knife (you do not need to do the paddle move here because there are three pieces on each side of the knife. It is best to use it anyway for the sake of continuity of movement).
5. Remove the pieces from one side of the knife and discard them so the blade is now clean. Using the Paddle Move again, show that the pieces of napkin have also vanished from the other side.
6. With a snap of the fingers you can now make the napkin pieces re-appear on the blade. All you have to do is roll the handle between your finger and thumb to turn the blade over, cover this rolling action with a shake of the hand and it will not be seen. The sudden appearance of the three coloured pieces of napkin will be quite a surprise.
7. To add to the surprise, do the Paddle Move one more time and show that the three pieces have also returned to the other side.

This trick is often performed as the 'salt spot trick'. The moves are identical to the above trick but instead of using pieces of paper napkin, salt is used. To get the salt to stick to the knife wet the end of your finger and touch the knife blade in the three places where you want the salt to stick. Shake some salt onto the damp area of the blade and tip off any excess. I have tried both versions and can't decide which one is best, so play with them both and decide which one you prefer.

SHIRTLESS

This is a party stunt that will always get a great response. Imagine walking into a party and after chatting to a couple of people taking hold of someone's shirt and pulling it off – without removing their jacket or damaging the shirt!

Versions of this trick have been performed by many famous magicians from Tommy Cooper to Harry Blackstone Jnr. Why not add your name to the list?

METHOD

The secret of this trick is that you are using a stooge. Get a friend to put on a shirt without putting his arms down the sleeves. At this stage it will look a little odd but if you do up the top three buttons and then put a jacket on and fasten the buttons of the jacket, all will look normal. To get maximum impact you should make sure that everyone is watching. Undo the buttons and with one sharp tug the shirt will come free. Pull it straight up and out of the top of the jacket. Make sure that your stooge acts surprised as his reaction will add to the overall effect.

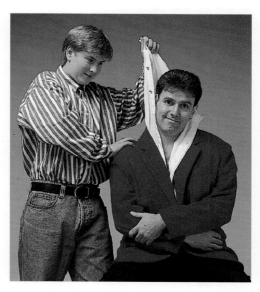

Above: Undo the top buttons and with one sharp pull someone at the party will be shirtless!

To get ready, place the shirt loosely over the shoulders and do up the top three buttons. Put on the jacket and then tuck in the sleeves.

D.I.Y. MAGIC

What is "Do It Yourself" magic? Many tricks are performed with ordinary objects. Sometimes we cheat and do some secret preparation before the audience sees the trick, and sometimes the trick needs a special prop to make it work. The tricks in this chapter all need a simple prop to be made or some secret preparation which you can do yourself. Using some sticky-backed plastic, a few pieces of card, some glue and a few other bits and bobs you can find around the house, you will be able to do miracles.

Many magicians have invented astounding tricks by playing around with ideas at home. Robert Harbin invented the trick known as the Zig-Zag Lady, where his assistant would stand in an upright cabinet. Then she was divided into three pieces and the middle portion slid out to the side. Beautifully presented expensive versions of this illusion have been performed all over the world but the prototype of this trick was built out of cardboard in his garage !

The following tricks are not as complicated as the Zig-Zag Lady but they can all be made with no special skills so don't panic if you do not consider yourself a D.I.Y. handyman or woman, just remember that the best magic of all is being able to say 'I made that'.

THE UNBURSTABLE BALLOON

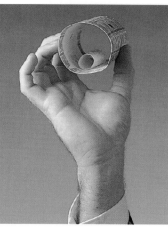

A long balloon is dropped through a tube and inflated so that it is clearly seen sticking out of the top and bottom of the tube. You hypnotize the balloon and tell it that it will feel no pain. Two sharp kebab skewers are then thrust through the balloon but to the surprise of the audience it doesn't burst.

Remember that some children can be frightened by balloons bursting. The point of magic is to entertain people, so be aware of the feelings of your audience.

PREPARATION

The prop you will need to construct for this trick is really 2 tubes. The outer tube is 12cm (4³/₄in) high and 6cm (2¹/₂in) in diameter. The inner tube is 3cm long and 2cm in diameter. You will also need some long airship balloons. The tubes shown in the picture were made from cardboard and covered in sticky-backed plastic but you could use any suitably sized cylinder. For example, cut the top and bottom off of a washing-up liquid bottle and you will have an excellent outer tube. The small tube must be glued or taped in the centre of the larger tube and then, using one of the skewers, make 4 holes in the outer tube so that they will pass through the centre of the outer tube and miss the inner tube completely.

The performance of this trick is very easy as the prop does all the work for you. Always pre-blow the balloons before the performance, they are a lot easier to blow up second time around. Remember to avoid allowing spectators to see inside the tube or they will work out how the trick is done. Once the balloon is in place and inflated the small tube will be hidden from all angles.

PERFORMANCE

Drop the end of the balloon through both tubes (it must go through the smaller tube as it is this that protects the balloon) and inflate it so that it is visible at the top and the bottom of the tube.

When the balloon is inflated you will need to tie a knot in the end. If you tie a slip knot, one tug on the end of the

Above: An inside view showing the inner tube which protects the balloon from the deadly skewers

balloon at the end of the trick and you can deflate it and hand it out for examination. If you prefer to tie a normal knot, then you will have to burst the balloon to get it out of the tube – there's nothing like finishing with a bang !

Now it's time for you to do some acting. Build the suspense before sticking the skewers through the balloon by pretending to be afraid (maybe you could give out ear plugs !) Then push the skewers through, do it slowly, pretend that it takes some effort. When the second skewer is through you can then show from all sides how the balloon has been pierced but has not burst.

AN ALTERNATIVE

For another balloon-puncturing trick, blow up a round balloon and then stick two pieces of clear sticky tape on opposite sides of it. Using a long sharp needle you will be able to penetrate the tape and the

Left: When the balloon is fully inflated it will fill the tube, and hide the inner tube from the audience.

Below: Sticking the skewers through the balloon.

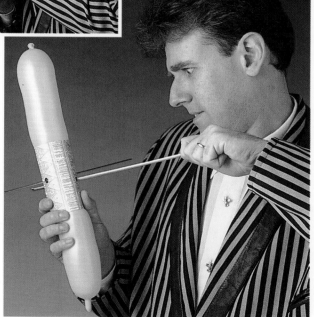

balloon will not burst. If your needle is long enough you can feed it out through the other side of the balloon. Make sure you hit the sticky tape on the other side of the balloon or the trick will end sooner than you expect.

CLIPPO

A strip of newspaper is shown, it is one column wide and about 40cm(16in) long. The magician explains that they are all adverts but most of them are of no interest – but hang on a second, this advert is for a very nice car, and it's very cheap. Fold the paper in half, pick up the scissors and cut it out from the strip. As you re-read the advert the strip of paper falls open and it is still in one piece. You explain that you can't drive so you will need to get some learner plates. Fold the strip in half, make another cut, and the strip is now restored but as an 'L' shape.

PREPARATION

Cut a long strip of small ads out of a local newspaper. One side of the paper is treated in the following way: Put a thin layer of rubber cement or contact adhesive over the central 20cm of the paper and allow it to dry thoroughly (at least 15 minutes). When that is done, gently rub some talcum powder all over the glued area – this will prevent the glue sticking to itself when the paper is folded in half. The glued side of the paper will be a slightly different colour from the other side but in performance this is not seen by the audience. It is a great trick so don't just make one, make several, they keep for a long time and still work.

PERFORMANCE

Before you cut the paper you must make sure that it is folded with the glued side on the inside of the fold. As the paper (and glue) is cut, the glue comes in contact with itself and sticks together immediately. Make the fold and the cut as straight as possible by following a line of type. After cutting out a small piece let the strip fall open and it will be back in one long strip.

The finale of the trick is to cut the paper so it ends up in the 'L' shape. To do this fold the paper in half as you did earlier and instead of making a straight cut, make the cut at an angle of 45°. It is a trick that can really send you round the bend!

In performance you may want to cut

Above: 'This advert looks interesting!'

Right: Fold the strip with the prepared side on the inside.

Above: As you read the advert, let the strip casually drop open.

You don't need to buy 'L' plates if you are magicians.

and restore the paper a number of times. You can repeat the trick but remember that each time you make a cut you are cutting away some of the glued portion of the paper. When all the glue is cut away the trick will no longer work.

To make sure that the paper is not examined by anyone when you finish the trick, screw the paper up into a ball, and throw it away.

THE CHANGE BAG

The change bag is one of the most versatile props available to a magician. It is not a trick in itself but a prop that is used for many different tricks. The bag is used to secretly exchange one item or items for another. You can use rope, coins, playing cards, coloured ping-pong balls, or anything that fits in the bag. Details of a couple of tricks are shown below but let's first learn how a simple cloth bag can be used to make magic.

HOW IT WORKS

Unbeknown to the audience the bag is divided into 2 sections or 'pockets'. It is these pockets that make the bag work. During a trick, objects are switched by placing them into one pocket and taking the other item out of the other pocket. Never let the audience examine the bag or they will discover the secret.

Above: The two sections (or pockets) of the change bag. This view of the bag is not for the eyes of the audience.

HOW TO MAKE A CHANGE BAG

The overall size of the finished bag should be approximately 30cm (12in) deep and 20cm (8in) wide. Cut 3 pieces of black lining material a little larger than the size of the bag and place them on top of one another. Sew round three of the sides leaving the fourth side open. The hems of the open side will need to be folded and

sewn to stop them fraying. This will be the lining of the bag and the secret workings.

To finish the bag, give it a magical look. Decorate the outside by cutting out and sewing on some brightly coloured stars or cover it completely with a patterned material as I have done. A well-made change bag will last a long time, so it is worth making a nice one.

PERFORMANCE

In this first routine with the change bag we are going to use it to magically knot and unknot some handkerchiefs. To do this you will need two sets of matching colourful hankies. The first set is knotted and secretly hidden in the rear pocket of

the change bag. The second set are placed singly in the front pocket.

To perform the trick, pick up the bag and openly remove the single handkerchiefs from the front pocket. Turn the bag inside out so that the empty front pocket ends up on the outside. While doing this, keep the secret entrance to the other pocket away from the audience. To all intents and purposes you have shown the bag to be completely empty.

Turn the bag back so it is right side out and openly place the single handkerchiefs back in the front pocket of the bag. Now to do some magic. Wave your wand or make a magic pass with your hand. Reach into the rear pocket of the back and slowly pull out the knotted handkerchiefs. You can then show the bag empty again by turning it inside out by using the rear pocket. By reversing the process you can also make the knots disappear!

Left: Turning the bag inside-out.

Below: Placing handkerchiefs in the bag.

THE CUT AND RESTORED TIE

This is one of my favourite tricks. Imagine the fun you can have at a party by going up to the host and after announcing that you are going to do some magic, cutting his tie in half! This is only the beginning. Keep cutting until his tie is in several pieces and then offer to restore it using your magic bag.

The bag is shown empty, the pieces are placed inside, you wave your magic wand, you reach inside and remove . . . a tie cut into several pieces. Oh no, the trick has gone wrong, but before you are thrown out of the party you have a second try and manage to restore the tie to a thunderous round of applause from the other guests.

PREPARATION

You will need a change bag and 2 matching ties. One of the ties is put in the rear section of the bag and the other must be worn by your volunteer/victim. To get the tie around his neck you have two alternatives. You can ask him in advance and tell him to act surprised when you cut the tie, or, if you have a wicked streak, get a friend to give him the tie as a present and make sure he puts it on. This way he will be genuinely surprised when you eventually cut the tie (his new present!) and very relieved when it is restored. This trick is ideal for performance at Christmas or on birthdays when presents are usually given.

PERFORMANCE

The pictures tell the story. All you have to remember is to show the bag empty by turning it inside out as described earlier. Then put the cut pieces of tie in the front section of the bag. To add a little drama to the trick wave your hands over the bag, say

Above: The victim will be very surprised when you boldly cut his tie in half!

Above: If you're going to do anything you might as well do it properly, so cut the tie into many pieces!

Right: The tie is restored to the relief of the victim and the amazement of the audience.

the magic words and remove the cut pieces of tie. After apologizing profusely you have another go, this time you remove the restored tie from the bag which you again show to be empty.

OTHER TRICKS WITH A CHANGE BAG

The cut and restored tie routine can be performed with a handkerchief. Borrow one from a spectator and after cutting it in half it can be

Left: By now his surprise will have gone and he will be entering a state of shock!

restored in the bag. The use of the change bag is only limited by your imagination. A rope can become knotted or unknotted, Two pieces of rope can be joined together, ribbon loops can be magically linked. Put your mind to work and see if you can come up with your own ideas.

THE DEVIL'S HANKY

This is another magician's prop which will help you do many tricks. It is a gimmicked hanky that will make vanish a key, a ping-pong ball, or any small item that you wrap in its folds. In this example we are using it to make a coin disappear but the moves are the same whatever you are using. The great thing about it is that the spectator can be holding the item that is about to disappear up until the very last moment. One second it is there, the next it is gone!

HOW IT WORKS

The hanky is in fact two identical hankies that have been sewn together. It is best to use colourful ones as these help to disguise the fact that it is a 'trick hanky' by hiding any give away lumps in the hanky after it has been made to vanish. Three sides are fully sewn but the fourth side is only sewn to the half way point. This provides us with an entrance to a secret pocket within the hanky and anything placed in this pocket will vanish. Note the coloured bead that is attached to the corner. This helps to locate the opening during performance. Obviously, we have to be a little clever to get our coin into the secret pocket, so follow the moves detailed below carefully and no-one will catch on that you are not using a normal hanky.

Remember that at the end of the trick the vanished item will still be in the hanky – don't let anyone pick it up after the trick. If you remove it from your pocket at the start of the trick and pop it back when you have finished, no-one will suspect that it is anything other than normal.

PERFORMANCE

At the start of the trick the Devil's Hanky will be in your pocket and the item to be made to vanish will be in the hands of a member of the audience. Fold the hanky into quarters so that the corner with the bead is at the front (away from your body) and hold it by the corners in your left hand.

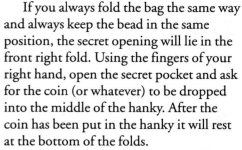

Above: The Devil's Hanky – an inside view.

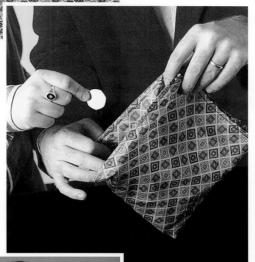

Right: The spectator can drop the coin, or whatever, into the folded hanky (actually into the bag) so he has no doubt that it is in there.

Above: Give the coin to the spectator to hold through the hanky. He put it in, he is holding it, surely you cannot make it disappear.

Right: Tug the coin free and it will remain hidden in the hanky. Hold the hanky by the top and show both sides – it has vanished.

If you always fold the bag the same way and always keep the bead in the same position, the secret opening will lie in the front right fold. Using the fingers of your right hand, open the secret pocket and ask for the coin (or whatever) to be dropped into the middle of the hanky. After the coin has been put in the hanky it will rest at the bottom of the folds.

Let the member of the audience feel the coin so they are sure that it is in the hanky. Then suggest that they hold on to the coin so it will be safe and will not get lost. After all, you can't be too careful. If you wish to, you can shake some magic salt or wave your magic wand over the coin. This has no effect whatsoever, but magicians do that sort of thing!

Now to actually make the coin vanish. You have done all the hard work by positioning the coin in the secret pocket. All you have to do is take hold of the hanky by the corner with the bead, this keeps the opening at the top and stops the coin falling on the floor after. One quick pull so the hanky/coin is dropped by the spectator and the coin will have disappeared! Casually show the hanky on both sides and replace it in your pocket to hide the evidence.

THE SQUARE CIRCLE PRODUCTION BOX

This nifty little prop will enable you to produce a lot of coloured handkerchiefs, a pile of sweets, or even a teddy bear. Depending on the size of the prop that you make you could even use it to produce your assistant – but to do this you would need to make a very large box (or have a very small assistant). The production box that we have shown is only 15cm (6in) high, but the principle is exactly the same whatever size you make.

HOW IT WORKS

The square circle production box consists of three parts although the audience are only ever made aware of two of them.

The 'square' or the outer box is a patterned box with some 'windows' cut in one side. These windows allow the audience to see into the box from the front. The inside of this box must be matt black, either painted or lined with black cartridge paper. My box was simply made from cardboard and then covered in sticky-backed plastic to give it a nice finish.

The 'circle' is a brightly coloured tube that nests snugly in the outer box. It can be made from card or if you want it to be more solid, use a large can with the top and bottom removed. If you are using a can, be aware that some can openers leave sharp edges, make sure these are filed off and covered with thick tape. Decorate the tube so that it will be clearly seen through the windows of the outer box when they are nested together.

The final part is the load chamber, a slightly smaller tube that will fit inside the 'circle'. It must be painted matt black or

covered with cartridge paper to match the inside of the 'square'. The size of this inner tube will dictate the size of the things you are going to produce.

The box works because of a principle that magicians call black on black. The load chamber can be filled to the brim with goodies and then placed in the 'square'. If you look through the windows in the outer box the eye will think it is seeing the back of the box. Remember that the audience will not be aware of the existence of the load chamber, so will have no doubt that the outer box is empty, especially when you demonstrate this by following the sequence shown below.

PERFORMANCE

The three pieces are nested together at the start of the trick, the load chamber is in position and, in this case, is full of coloured silk hankies. Note that the load chamber is invisible due to the black on black principle. The only thing to remember when performing this trick is that a view from the top will give the secret away. Make sure that the audience are seated and cannot see into the top of the box before you start.

The sequence of moves to show that the box is empty is as follows: Pick up and display the box (square), apparently empty, show the tube (circle) to be empty, insert it in an out of the box to show box empty, replace it in box and start the production.

Above: **Keep this view hidden from the spectators.**

Centre: **Nothing in the tube.**

Below: **Nothing in the box.**

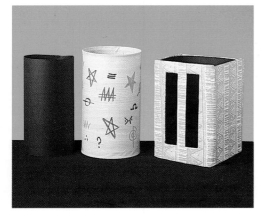

Left: **The secret workings of the box.**

Right: **So where do these come from?**

THE HANDKERCHIEF PULL

One of the most effective tricks a magician can perform is to make something disappear and there are many ways of doing this. The handkerchief pull is a device that will let you make a hanky vanish without using any visible props and end up with your hands really empty. The device that is used for this effect is ingenious because while doing all the work for you, it remains hidden from the audience. It is also simple to make and use!

HOW TO MAKE A PULL

A pull works by pulling the item to be vanished out of your hands and hiding it under your jacket. It consists of two safety pins, a piece of elastic that is about 30cm (12in) long and an empty plastic 35mm-film canister. White elastic has been used in the illustrations so that it can be seen more clearly but black elastic should be used as it will be less visable. Tie the first safety pin (the anchor) onto the end of the elastic, then thread the second safety pin (the runner) onto the elastic using the round 'eye' of the pin. To complete the pull you must connect it to the film canister. Make a small hole in the bottom of the canister and feed the elastic through, tie a small washer on the end of the elastic to stop it passing back through the hole.

The pull is worn around your waist so that the canister hangs on your right side. The runner pin is pinned to your waistband in the position shown and the anchor pin

is taken round your back and fastened so that the elastic is tight enough to hold the canister in position. Do not pull the elastic too tight or you will not be able to use the pull when you need it. Now put a jacket on to hide the apparatus and put a hanky in your left trouser pocket and you are ready to start the performance.

PERFORMANCE

The first stage in using the pull is to secretly get the canister into your right hand. To do this, place both your hands in your trouser pockets as if you are looking for your hanky, take the hanky out of your left pocket with your left hand and bring you right hand forward in a fist which contains the canister, open side to the top. The elastic will not be seen as long as you keep the back of your hand to the audience

and your arm close to your body so the elastic runs along your arm and under the jacket.

Now push the hanky down into the canister so that no loose ends are trailing out of your hand. By simply letting the canister slip through your fingers it will be pulled under your jacket and out of sight, the hanky will have vanished. Make sure you keep your arm close to your body or the canister will catch on your jacket and the audience may notice it.

PERFORMANCE TIP Do not rush to open your hand and show that the hanky has disappeared. As far as the audience is concerned you must still be holding the hanky in your hand even after the pull has done its work. Act as if you are still holding the hanky wrapped into a tight ball. Ask someone to blow on your hand, then slowly open your hand to show that it is empty.

Left: Do not move your hand too far away from your body or someone may notice the elastic.

Below: When the hanky has been pushed into the canister let the elastic pull it out of sight.

Left: The pull in position on the waistband. Make sure that it does not pull too tight

THE CHINESE COMPASS

The Chinese have a reputation for being clever and this trick is just that, very clever. It is also very simple, the kind of trick that you can perform at any time and any place. It is a perfect pocket trick as it is a small prop that you can carry with you at all times.

The Chinese compass is octagonal in shape and it has an arrow or a pointer on both sides. This is shown to the audience and they notice that the arrow points the same way on both sides. You tell the story of a traveller who stole the compass from a powerful magus. The compass was meant to be magic and would always point in the direction of buried treasure. The traveller decided to seek his fortune with the compass and as the story unfolds the arrows keep magically changing direction. When the magus discovered the theft he cast a spell so that without the magic words the compass was worthless. The traveller never did make his fortune. He threw the compass away and that is how you come to have it, and it still doesn't work! As you finish the story you give the compass out for examination and whenever someone turns it it points in a different direction.

Above: Hold the compass between finger and thumb and use your other hand to swivel it round.

Left: Experiment by holding a different pair of corners and see where the arrow points.

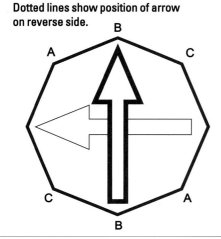

Dotted lines show position of arrow on reverse side.

HOW IT WORKS

The compass is made by cutting an octagonal about 5cm (2in) in diameter from a piece of thick card. Two arrows are drawn, one on each side of the compass, they must be at right angles to each other (see illustration). To make the compass needles point in opposite directions the thumb and forefinger of the left hand hold the points marked C, use the right hand to turn the compass without changing the grip of the left hand. To make the needles point the same way hold the compass at the points marked a and turn the compass as before. The final variation is to hold the compass at the points marked B and the needle will point in opposite directions on either side. Armed with this knowledge and a little practice you are in complete control of the compass and can make the needles point in whichever direction you please. When a spectator tries they will have no control over the direction of the arrows.

THE AFGHAN BANDS

The magician asks for the help of a spectator and hands him three strips of crêpe paper, each strip having been glued together at the ends to form a large loop. The magician and spectator take a loop each and the other is set aside. 'What would happen if one of the loops was cut in half?' asks the magician. The answer is obvious, you would end up with two separate loops. This can be checked by cutting a loop in half which is exactly what the magician does. Now the spectator is challenged to do the same thing, nothing could be easier. But when he tries he ends up with two loops that are linked! The only way to separate them is by breaking the loops. He is given a second chance but this time he ends up with only one loop, but it is twice the size that it was at the start. This is a colourful and baffling illusion that is fun to do and can involve a number of people. In another presentation you could give out a number of loops and all the girls discover that when cut they have two linked loops and all the boys have large loops. Only the magician ends up with two separate loops. The magic happens in the hands of the spectators so no-one can accuse you of cheating.

HOW IT WORKS

There are three different types of loop in this trick. Each one is made from a strip of coloured crêpe paper 10cm (4in) wide by 2 metres (80in) long.

LOOP A : The first loop is the one that divides into two separate loops. To make this loop take the strip of crêpe paper and glue the ends together. Make sure that there are no twists in the strip of paper before you glue it together.

LOOP B : This loop becomes one large loop when cut in half. To make this loop put a half twist (180°) in the strip before glueing the ends together. The loops are nice and long so this will not be noticed when it comes to cutting them in half.

LOOP C : This loop divides into two loops that are linked. It is made in the same way as loop B only this time put a full twist (360°) in the strip before glueing the ends together.

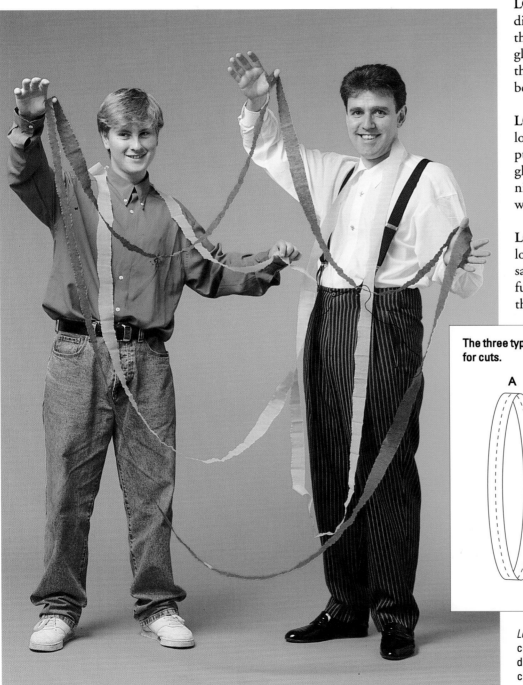

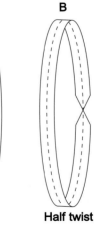 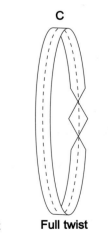

The three types of loop, showing twists and dotted lines for cuts.

A   B   C

Half twist   Full twist

Left: Make the trick colourful by using different coloured crêpe paper strips and you have an effect that will fill the stage.

Above: Cut along the dotted lines and the magic happens right in your hands.

THE SPOT PADDLES

Two plastic paddles are shown, one has a spot on both sides and the other is blank on both sides. As the paddles are shown the spots seem to appear and disappear at the whim of the magician. Just when someone thinks they might know what is happening the spots jump off one paddle and there are now four spots on the other ! Another great pocket trick, they take up no space and can be slipped in a purse or wallet and be ready to use at any time.

THE PADDLES

The paddles can be made out of thick card but ideally should be made from plastic. (Sheets of plastic of business/letter/A4 size are available from model and craft shops). Plastic paddles last longer and handle better and should be made from plastic 3mm (¼in). The dimensions of my paddles are as follows: total length 14cm (5½in), length of handle 5cm (2in), width 3cm (2⅜in), width of handle 0.5cm (7/16in). The spots can be drawn on with a permanent marker or cut out of sticky-backed plastic. The arrangement of the spots is as follows: paddle A has one spot on one side and the other side is left blank; paddle B has one spot on one side and two spots on the other side.

THE PADDLE MOVE

This move is designed to look as if you are showing both sides of a paddle when in reality you are showing the same side twice. The move is broken down into three stages and when put together in a smooth flowing action is one hundred per cent effective.

1. Hold the paddle in the right hand with the thumb on top and the fingers underneath. The paddle should be pointing away from you and angled down so that the audience can clearly see the face up side.

2. Roll the handle of the paddle between the thumb and fingers so that the paddle is turned over to display the other side. This is done by sliding the thumb to the left and pulling the fingers back to the right.

Left: 1. The starting point for the paddle move. The fingers should form a flat bed on which the handle is rolled.

Right: 2. Half way through the move. When performed as one this stage is never seen, the larger wrist action hides the small rolling movement of the thumb.

Left: 3. The end of the move. Note the position of the hand in relation to the body is the same.

Below: 4. With a flick of the wrist (and a roll of the thumb) the spots can be made to jump from paddle to paddle. You can also do the paddle move from this position – roll the fingers and thumb to turn over the paddles and at the same time, turn your hand over by twisting at the wrist.

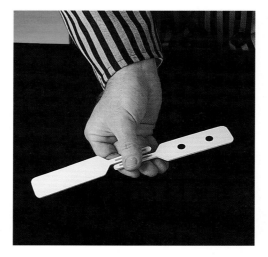

3. Twist the wrist so that the paddle is pointing upwards and the side that was underneath is now shown to the audience. This last stage does not involve raising the arm, the hand should remain the same distance from your body.

Follow the above moves through the three stages shown in photographs 1, 2 and 3. Start off slowly doing each stage separately, then reverse the order of the stages, starting at 3 and going back to 1. When you have mastered each stage individually it is time to put them together and perform the whole action as one continuous movement. Hold the paddle as in stage 1 and roll the paddle (stage 2) and twist the wrist (stage 3) at the same time. Now reverse the process combining the roll and the twist to return to the starting position. You will probably surprise yourself with the illusion. You will see the same side twice while giving the impression of showing both sides.

When you have mastered the move with your right hand it is time to learn it with your left. It is also possible to do the move with both paddles in one hand, not essential, but it is fun to do.

PERFORMANCE

In performance you start with a paddle in each hand, paddle A (blank side up) is in your right hand and paddle B (single spot up) is in your left. Both paddles are shown using the paddle move to be identical on both sides, ie. paddle A is shown blank and paddle B has a single spot on each side.

You are now going to make a spot appear on the paddle in your right hand (paddle A). Touch the underside of paddle A with the top side of paddle B and then show both sides of paddle A, only this time do not do the paddle move – miss out stage 2 of the move and you really do show both sides. The spot has appeared on paddle A. Turn the paddle A over so that the spot side is face up and repeat the move so that both paddles can now be shown to have one spot on each side.

You can shake the spots off paddle A by giving a quick flick of the wrist and starting the above sequence again. Then as a finale you can make both spots jump onto one paddle. Hold the paddles (both showing a single spot) as in figure 4. Flick the wrist in the direction of paddle B and at the same time roll the handles of the paddle as if you were doing the paddle move. This will give the illusion that the spot has jumped from one paddle to the other – leaving your audience with spots before their eyes!

THE VANISHING COAT-HANGER

A wire coat-hanger is wrapped in a piece of newspaper which is immediately screwed up into a tight ball to show that the coat-hanger has vanished. This can also be performed as a show of strength by getting a member of the audience to try and do as you do. You will screw your wrapped-up hanger into a small ball whereas a member of the audience will just end up folding it in half and then struggling with it to make it smaller.

METHOD

The secret is in the coat-hanger. It looks normal but instead of being made from stiff wire it is made from solder. Solder is very pliable so that when it is folded up in the newspaper it will crush easily and you will look as if you have great strength.

Left: Fold all the edges in to make a neat little package.

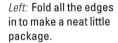

Above: Casually screw up the paper – and apparently the coat-hanger.

Above: Make it obvious that the coat-hanger is going in the middle of the sheet of newspaper.

Left: Throw away the paper, dust off your hands, and on to the next trick!

HEADS I WIN, TAILS YOU LOSE

Have you ever been had? Isn't it annoying when someone comes up to you and starts a sentence with the words 'I bet you can't...' The chances are that you have just been challenged with an impossible task, or there is a trick involved. Whatever the situation you know you are going to lose.

Some tricks of this nature are used on street corners to get money out of naive strangers. You have probably heard of Three Card Monte (also known as Find the Lady or Chase the Ace). In this trick three cards are casually thrown onto a table and all you have to do is find the money card. Do not try and play this game as you cannot win – it is a con. As is the game where there are three walnut shells and a pea. Trying to make money with bets like these is illegal in all countries, but you can still have fun by trying some of the challenges in this chapter on your friends. But be ready to run when they realize that they too have been had!

THE ONE GLASS CHALLENGE

Place a glass full of your favourite drink on the table and cover it with a paper bag. Tell your victim that you are going to drink the contents of the glass without touching the paper bag. Impossible, he will cry.

What you do is crawl under the table and pretend that you have taken the glass through a trap door in the table. Make slurping noises as if you are drinking and then come out from under the table. Your friend will not be impressed and when he picks up the paper bag to check you calmly reach forward, pick up the glass and drink the drink.

You have now done exactly what you said you would do – you drank the drink without touching the paper bag.

THE THREE GLASS CHALLENGE

Three glasses are set up on the table, two of them are faced one way and the middle one is the other way up. Show the audience that it is possible to turn all the glasses so that they are all the right way up. You have to turn two glasses at a time and all they have to do is copy you. Get them to watch you very carefully as you demonstrate. No matter how many times you show them the glasses will always end up upside-down when they try.

HOW?

Look at the directions of the glasses in the first picture, the start, and the last picture which is how your victim starts. Do you see the difference? It is impossible to get the three glasses the right way up using these moves unless the glasses are the same way up as they are in the first picture. The last move of turning over the centre glass for the victim to try results in the glasses being the opposite way up to how they were when you started.

Left: **1:** Pick up the middle glass in your right hand and the left hand glass in your left hand and turn them over.

Below: **2:** Pick up the two end glasses and turn them over.

Right: **3:** As in move 1 pick up the middle glass with your right hand and the left glass with your left hand and turn them over.

Above: The result of the three moves is three glasses, all the right way up.

Right: Now turn the middle glass over and ask the spectator to do exactly what you have just done. When he tries all the glasses will end up face down!

THE FIVE GLASS CHALLENGE

Five glasses are placed in a row, the first is empty, the next three are full, the last is also empty. Challenge someone to re-arrange the glasses so that they are alternately empty and full – but they are only to touch one glass.

Below: The picture tells the story, all you have to do is pick up the middle glass, drink the contents and then replace it!

THE BOTTLE AND STRAW CHALLENGE

You will find people give up on this one very quickly! The challenge is to pick up a bottle with an ordinary drinking straw. They are not allowed to touch or move the bottle, they just have to lift it up off the table using the straw.

HOW? Bend the straw in half and lower it into the bottle. When the straw gets past the neck it will spring out and hook the bottle and it will be a simple matter to lift it up off the table. If the straw straightens out in the bottle then the bend must be further up the straw.

BLOW OVER A BOTTLE

To start this challenge you will need to have a bottle in a paper bag. Take out the bottle and put it on the table. Put the paper bag down and challenge your victim to blow the bottle over. Try as he might the bottle will not budge.

HOW? Place the bottle on the corner of the paper bag and then blow into the bag. The bottle will topple over as the bag inflates. This can also be performed with a house brick, book or any other heavy object. WARNING: Be very careful if using a bottle as it could topple over, roll onto the floor and break.

CLIMBING THROUGH A BIRTHDAY CARD

Did you know that it is possible to cut a hole in a birthday card that is big enough to climb through? Challenge a friend to do this and he will fail. Follow the instructions below and you will succeed.

Above: With the birthday card still folded in half, cut it as in the picture. Ten cuts will be more than enough.

Above: Open out the fold and cut along the crease. Do not cut the crease at the two ends or you will end up with two pieces rather than a hole.

Carefully open up the card and you will have a ring of card that is large enough to step through.

THE BANANA SURPRISE

This is more of a stunt than a trick but it never fails to get a good laugh. Imagine the reaction when someone peels a banana only to discover that it has already been neatly sliced.

HOW? Insert a needle into the banana and move back and forwards across the fruit. Bananas are very soft and this action will slice one without any effort. Repeat this down the whole banana depending on how many slices you want. Then replace the fruit in the bowl and wait for the fun.

How on earth did that happen ?

CHINESE HANDCUFFS

This stunt is great fun at parties as everyone can have a go. You need two pieces of rope each about 60cm (24in) long and two willing volunteers. Tie the ends of the ropes around the wrists so that the pair are linked together as shown and see if they can separate themselves without untying the ropes.

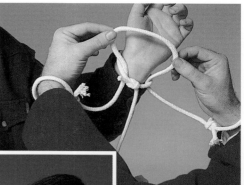

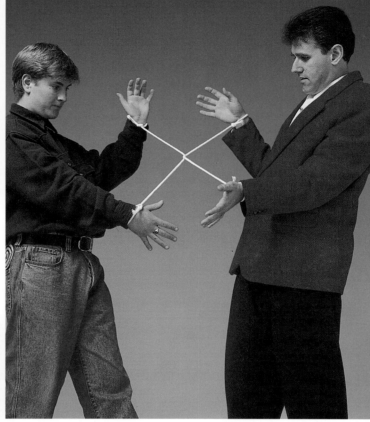

HOW: To separate the ropes you need to use the loop that goes around the wrists. Tuck the centre of your rope through the inside of the loop around your partner's wrist. Make a large loop and slip it over your partner's hand. The ropes should then be pulled tight and you will be free of each other.

Left: Many contortions will be tried before they give up! But unless they already know the secret they will fail.

SDRAWKCAB KCIRTA

Yes, it is an unpronounceable title! It is 'a trick backwards' spelt backwards. And this is a fun little interlude that everyone will want to try. Give each person in the room a piece of card and a pen. Ask them to hold the card on their forehead and then to write their name on the card. You will be surprised to see that nine out of ten people write their names in mirror writing (backwards and inside out). But the people who write their names backwards will be even more surprised, because they will not realize what they have done until they look at the cards.

If you try this on yourself you will probably write your name in the normal way, this is because you know what to expect. Try it on someone else and both of you will be amazed at the effect.

MIND READING AND MATHEMATICAL MAGIC

If you were alive three hundred years ago and performed some of the tricks in this book you would probably have been convicted of being a witch and punished accordingly. Nowadays people are not quite so scared (or impressed) by conjuring, they are happy to regard our miracles as mere tricks. This is not the case for magic that is presented as mentalism.

Mentalism is the term that magicians use for tricks that involve mind reading or effects that involve Extra Sensory Perception (E.S.P.) Most of us would like to believe that our minds are more powerful than we think and all that we need to do is unlock the power that lies within. This may or may not be true, I have no way of proving or disproving the existance of E.S.P. But I can duplicate the effects of mind readers by using simple trickery.

In this chapter you will learn some easy-to-do effects that will impress your audience at the same time crediting you with superior mental powers. If you wish people to think of you as a mind reader, then do not let them see you doing other tricks as they will quickly make the link between the two, and in no time your mind reading will be just another trick.

THE MAGIC SQUARE

Wouldn't it be great if alongside your magical ability you had increased your mind power as well ? Performing this feat will have people thinking you are a mathematical genius as well as a master magician. What you do is ask a member of the audience to call out a number betweeen 25 and 75. Then, using your incredible mathematical skills (joke – you don't need any!) you immediately and without hesitation write out a four by four magic square for that number.

A magic square is a grid of numbers that adds up to the same amount along all the rows and columns. Here is an example of the magic square you would write if the number selected was 34.

8	11	14	1
13	2	7	12
3	16	9	6
10	5	4	15

This is a perfect magic square, get out your calculator and check if you want to. Every row and every column add up to 34 as do the diagonals. But it doesn't stop there. You can also reach the chosen number by any of the following ways.

1. Adding up the four corners
2. Divide the square into four quarters and then add up the four numbers in each corner (eg. 8,11,13,2, or 9,6,4,15)
3. The pan-diagonals also add up to 34 (13,11,6,4 and 14,12,3,5)
4. The top centre pairs and bottom centre pairs (11,14,5,4)
5. The side centre pairs (13,3,12,6)
Within the four by four square are four three by three squares and the corners of these add up to 34 as well (e.g. 8,14,3,9)
6. Any square of four numbers add up to 34.

This is just one example of a perfect magic square. You will be able to produce a similar magic square for any number between 25 and 75 and you will not have to memorize more than a simple system!

In the presentation that I have given below you do not even need to remember the key square that is the secret behind this mathemagical feat.

HOW IT WORKS
Creating a magic square for any number relies on a system and some simple maths. The first part of the system is known as the key square. By using the key square as a foundation you will be able to build a magic square for any number. By memorizing the key square you will be able to do the whole thing from memory.

8	11	B	1
A	2	7	12
3	D	9	6
10	5	4	C

To make the magic square work you have to replace the letters in the key square above with numbers that you must calculate in the following way.

A. This is the base number and is calculated by subtracting 21 from the chosen number. In the example given earlier the chosen number was 34. To find the base number we must subtract 21 from 34 to get a base of 13 which replaces the letter A. The rest of the numbers are a lot easier to calculate.

B. This number is the base number plus 1. So in our example where the base number is 13 the letter B is replaced by 13 + 1 which is 14.

C. This letter is replaced by the base number plus 2 (13 + 2) which is 15.

D. This letter is replaced by the base number plus 3 (13 + 3) which is 16.

PERFORMANCE
The best way to perform this effect is to memorize the key square and practice the calculations of the base number. With a little work you will be able to ask for a number between 25 and 75 then call out the sixteen numbers of the square. The person who chose the number can write them down as you call them out and then check the square to see if you are correct. I don't do it this way – but it is the best way.

Magicians achieve their tricks by cheating and I add a little extra cheating which means that I do not even need to remember the key square. To perform the trick my way you will need to draw or print a magic square grid on a postcard (I have the design shown printed on the back of a business card).

Fill in by hand all the numbers of the key square leaving the letter squares blank and keep the same pen that you used near to the card. To perform the trick all you need to do now is ask someone to name a number between 25 and 75 then write the chosen number in the box. A quick calculation as described above will give you the key number that is written in the blank space in the first column. The other blanks are quickly calculated and filled in and then I pretend to fill in all the other numbers. Make sure you use the same pen and that the numbers are all written in the same style. After the square is completed I give it out to be checked. By performing this you will quickly get a reputation for being a mathematical genius.

LIGHTNING ADDITION

This is a nifty piece of trickery that will help you demonstrate your highly tuned mind to anyone you choose. It takes almost no practice and no preparation and can be performed at any time. All you need is a piece of paper and a pen.

Ask a friend to write down two five digit numbers underneath each other. To this you add two five digit numbers of your own. Your friend then adds another number to the list. This gives you a list of five five digit numbers. Ask your friend how long it would take to add them up. Whatever he says you will be able to add them up in less time than it takes him to answer.

METHOD
The two numbers that you write down are directly related to the two numbers written by the friend who is helping with the trick. The numbers that you write down are the ones needed to add to the existing numbers to make 99999. This is best shown by an example.

If the first number written by your helper is 74635 then the number you need to write to go with this number is 25364.

$$74635$$
$$+ \underline{25364}$$
$$99999$$

This may sound difficult but it is not as all you need to do is look at each individual digit and write under it the number needed to make 9. Under a 7 you write a 2, under a 4 you write a 5, under a 9 you write 0. This procedure is carried out for the two numbers written by the helper giving you a list of four five digit numbers.

The final number should be written in a space that you leave between the two sets of numbers. This number will give you the key to the answer and as it will be similar to the final solution it is important that it is lost amongst the others. The final list may look something like this :

Spectator's 1st number
74635
Spectator's 2nd number
96439
Spectator's last number
48578
Your 1st number
25364
Your 2nd number
3560

To work out the total ignore all the numbers apart from the spectator's last number. Your answer must be a six digit number. The first digit will be a 2 followed by the first four digits of the spectator's last five digit number. The last digit is the last digit of the last number minus 2. In the example given above the correct answer is 248576. Check it out for yourself and then get someone to test your lightning mathematical ability.

MORE LIGHTNING ADDITION

A spectator is given a pad and asked to write down any two digits, one above the other. Then he is to add those two digits together and place the answer underneath the first two digits. Then he is to add the second and third numbers to arrive at a fourth number. This process is repeated until he has a vertical row of ten numbers. The result is called a Fibonacci sequence and if the two digits that you start with were 2 and 9 the sequence would look like this :

2
9
11
20
31
51
82
133
215
348

All these numbers are written down while your back is turned. When the list of ten numbers is complete you turn round and draw a line under the column and ask the spectator to add up the numbers. As soon as he starts adding up you call out the correct answer, and you only saw the list for a split second as you drew the line. After witnessing this trick you will find that spectators claim that you didn't even look at the numbers.

METHOD
To calculate the answer all you need to do is look at the number that lies fourth from the bottom and remember it – in our example that is the number 82. To work out the total of the column of numbers all you have to do is multiply this number by 11. Don't be put off thinking that you need to practise your 11 times table as there is an easy way to do this. First, multiply the number by 10 (i.e. add a zero to the end of the number 82 x 10 = 820) then add the number to your result (820 + 82 = 902). In the example above the sum of the numbers is 902.

PRESENTATION TIP
You could present this number juggling feat as a test of your memory. Have the numbers written down as described above and then get someone to show you the list of numbers for 2 seconds (this should give you ample time to locate and memorize the fourth number from the bottom). After being shown the list you can quickly calculate the sum of the numbers using the method described above. You can then announce that you have memorized the numbers and by using your brain as a calculator you know that the total is nine hundred and two. The audience will probably not believe you so you may need to have a calculator handy for them to check your answer!

THE MEMORY TEST

The effect that you can perform with this system is quite incredible: try it for yourself and even you will be amazed. We are going to give you the ability to memorize twenty random objects named by members of the audience, but not only that, you will also be able to recall that list in numerical order, in reverse order or name any item at any position in the list. This is a very impressive feat of mental agility and is not just a trick – it has many other uses in daily life. You can memorize a shopping list, key words for a speech or important facts for an exam.

To understand how memory tests work you will have to do some further reading, as that is beyond the scope of this book. We will, however, show you an application of a simple system that is perfectly suited to entertainment purposes. The first stage is to prove that the system works, and to do that you must take part in a simple test.

Below is a list of ten items. Look at the list for twenty seconds, and then close the book and try to list the items on a piece of paper.

1. telephone	5. suitcase	9. hat
2. book	6. scissors	10. radio
3. typewriter	7. pencil	
4. cards	8. curtains	

Well, how did you do? If you got seven or more you are doing quite well, but could you get them in the right order? Read the rest of this chapter and try the test at the end and you should achieve a score of ten out of ten – use an extended system, and you could remember hundreds of items.

THE PEG SYSTEM

The first job is to make sure that you actually organize your mind to take in the list. To do this, we are going to set up a list of twenty pegs which all have a number and a keyword name; these will all be easily remembered and become the hooks on which you will hang the items to remember.

The first ten items are easily remembered as they all rhyme with their numbers.

1. bun	5. hive	9. time
2. shoe	6. bricks	10. hen
3. tree	7. heaven	
4. door	8. gate	

Because of the rhyme you will find that these items can be memorized easily. This list will never change; the numbers and their names will be permanent. The next job is to learn to attach an object to a keyword. This is done by making a picture in your mind following the four rules below.

1. Be absurd
2. Exaggerate the picture
3. Substitute your items
4. Include movement where possible

Here are some examples using the list we gave you earlier. The first key word is 'bun' and the first item is a telephone; these items must be linked together following the rules given above. Try to imagine a telephone made to look like a sticky bun (substitution). You are trying to put down the hand piece but it has stuck to your hand (movement). Exaggerate the picture with your movements and build an absurd image in your mind. The word bun and telephone are now firmly linked.

Next, we have to link shoe (keyword) with book (object). Imagine that you are trying to put on your shoe, but you cannot get your foot into it because there is a book inside the shoe already! Or think of yourself lacing up a pair of books on your feet. Now, to link 'tree' and 'typewriter', imagine yourself as Newton standing under a tree just about to discover the law of gravity! Suddenly, a typewriter falls on your head. The more absurd the picture is the easier it is to recall. Go through the whole list, making up your own associations.

It is now time to try to recall the list of items one at a time. This is done in the following manner. Start with the number (e.g. number 1); this will lead your mind to the keyword (bun), which will remind you of the absurd picture of you on the telephone (or buniphone!). Try it for the rest of the list, and then try recreating the list forwards and backwards – easy, isn't it? If you want to surprise yourself put the book down for half an hour and try listing the words later – the pictures will remain with you far longer than they would if you had remembered a random list parrot-fashion. You will even be able to recall the list exactly in a few days' time.

EXTENDING THE SYSTEM

You can now extend the system to cover a list of twenty words by using another ten keywords for numbers eleven to twenty. Below is a list of keywords attached to numbers based on shapes; the number looks like the keyword.

1. pencil
2. swan
3. camel
4. sail boat
5. hook
6. golf club
7. boomerang
8. hourglass
9. tadpole
10. bat and ball

These keywords can be used to cover your second ten items. You now have a total of twenty keywords to use, so try the following experiment with your friends. It is ideal when they are pestering you for a trick or two as the performance can last for about ten minutes or more.

PRESENTATION FOR MEMORY MAGIC

You will need a pencil and paper so that your mental acrobatics can be checked by someone with a less agile mind! Proceed with the following patter:

'We are going to try an experiment to show how I have trained my mind to work for me. To double-check this, I need someone to write down a list of twenty items that you will all call out in a random order,' (give paper and pencil to someone). 'I want you all to memorize as many of the items as you can so that you can compare your performance with mine. When I say "Go" I want you to call out a random object and, when the item has been listed, a second and third until we have a list of twenty words on the paper,' (Say "Go", and start matching the objects to the keywords and making up absurd pictures).

'How many items do you think that you can recall? It is a little unfair, as you have only heard the list once; would you like to hear it again? Don't bother reading it, I'll do it.' (Go through your list of keywords and recall the complete list). 'Now who thinks they can do better?' (Get a volunteer to attempt to recall the list – as each item is called out image your

picture on fire, flames burning everything black, totally destroying the picture.) 'You missed out some of the items.' (Run through the list in your head and call out the number and the object word for every picture that is not 'burned').

To finish the routine, you can call the list out backwards by running through your keywords in reverse order. If you

want to know more about this and other techniques for remembering numbers, names, dates, etc., try a visit to your public library, where you will find books on memory techniques for many different situations and full explanations of how and why the systems work.

THE CHANGE ENVELOPE

The easiest way to read someone's mind is to tell them what to think of, and then pretend to mind read. This would not be very impressive so we need to dress up the scenario a little. To do this you will need to gimmick an envelope. The change envelope looks like an ordinary envelope but with it you can force a person to choose a particular word, card or number, and they will think that they had a free choice of many items when they only had a choice of one. Using this method many tricks are possible. In construction it is similar to a change bag (see page 37), but to use what is obviously a magician's prop is not a good idea if you are a mind reader. Use things that look ordinary and people will assume that they *are* ordinary.

HOW TO MAKE A CHANGE ENVELOPE

Take a large envelope, preferably made from good quality paper, and gently steam all the flaps open. Be very careful when doing this as the steam will burn your hands if you get too close. When this is done, open out the envelope and put it aside to dry thoroughly.

WARNING : STEAMING OPEN THE GLUED PART OF THE ENVELOPE IS DANGEROUS AND SHOULD NOT BE ATTEMPTED BY CHILDREN

Cut the back from a matching envelope to provide a piece of paper the same size as the envelope with no flaps attached. This will become the divider between the two pockets of the finished article.

Glue the divider into the opened out envelope with a good quality paper glue or contact adhesive. Put the glue along a 2cm strip at the bottom of the envelope. There is no need to stick the sides of the divider to the envelope.

Now glue the envelope back together so that it looks identical to a normal envelope. The divider may need to be trimmed slightly so that it cannot be seen

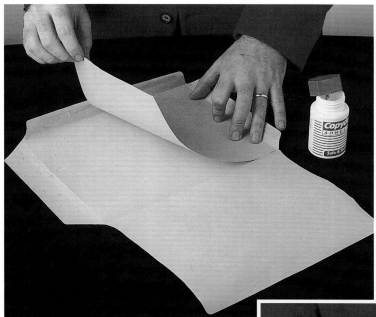

Left: Inserting the divider to make two pockets in the envelope. When the envelope is glued together the divider should not be visible.

Below: A change envelope – the inside view. When used the, divider will fall flat against the side and be undetected.

from the outside of the envelope. The divider will rest flat against either side of the envelope depending on which pocket is opened.

PERFORMANCE

To use a change envelope to force a number you will need about thirty small slips of paper. On fifteen of them write different numbers and place them in the back pocket of the change envelope. On the remaining fifteen slips write the same number, the one that you want to force and place them in the front pocket of the envelope. You are now ready to perform the force.

It is important that your spectators think that the choice is free, so at the start you can pick out a number of slips from the back pocket and have someone read them out. Replace all these slips in the back pocket and then give the envelope a good shake to mix them all around. Open the envelope and insert a couple of fingers in the front pocket. This will ensure that the dividing flap is pushed back and closes the back pocket. A spectator can now dip into the front pocket and select a single slip of paper which will bear the number that you wish to force.

Here are a couple of routines that use the change envelope, but with a bit of thought I am sure you will think of some of your own.

THE TRAVELLER'S DREAM

Members of the audience call out names of places that they would like to visit. The names are written on slips of paper and dropped into an envelope. Someone chooses a slip of paper from the envelope and you are able to read their mind to ascertain what is on the slip. This is no mean feat in itself but you then tell of a vivid dream you had last night. In that dream you were in a foreign country and you marked the place on an atlas. Pick up your atlas and show that the pages are unmarked. Then turn to the city that has been chosen and there is a large 'X' over the chosen city.

To prepare for this trick, have fifteen blank papers ready for the audience's suggestions and fifteen prepared papers that all say 'PARIS' loaded into the front of the change envelope. You will also need to mark an atlas with an 'X' over the French capital. When the audience has called out a number of cities and you have written them down, drop them in the back of the envelope. If no-one says Paris then you will need to pretend that you have heard it or just say it yourself, but don't worry, this has never happened to me yet! All that you have to do now is have a slip of paper selected from the front pocket and think of the city.

55

SPIRIT WRITING

This is a spooky trick which is great fun at a late night party, especially if people have been telling ghost stories. In this trick you are going to make a spooky message appear on a blank piece of paper. The paper and a pencil are placed into an envelope which is passed around the room. Everyone takes a turn at holding it and concentrating and then shaking the envelope. When the envelope is opened there is a scratchy message for one of the people in the room.

By now the method will be clear. You are using a change envelope to switch a blank piece of paper for one with a message on it. When you write the message, make sure it is very scratchy and has extra lines and dots over the page. To get maximum impact the message should be only just readable but remember not to frighten anyone too much – after all it's only for fun.

Turn your head and offer your volunteer a free choice. Note that a couple of fingers are in the envelope to hold the divider flat against the back of the envelope. There is now no chance of choosing from the wrong pocket.

SIMPLE PSYCHOMETRY

Do not try looking up the word psychometry in the dictionary to find out what it means – it will not be there! It is a word that has been made up by magicians to explain a pseudo-psychic phenomenon. According to magicians, psychometry is the art of sensing information from an inanimate object. As a bloodhound uses smell to locate the owner of an article of clothing, a psychometrist can ascertain information about a person by holding an object that belongs to that person. This is all a lot of gobbledygook but, luckily for us, most people seem to think it is true.

If you can act a little and play the part of a mind-reader convincingly then this trick is a lot of fun. Don't be put off by the method as it is the simplicity of the trick that deceives, not clever and devious magic.

After explaining to the audience that you have developed the skill of psychometry (and telling them all about it) you ask for five volunteers to help you in an experiment. Each volunteer is given an envelope and asked to place a personal item in it and to seal it down. Items like rings, watches, keys, anything that has been kept close to them for a period of time. The envelopes are collected and mixed up so that no-one can tell which envelope belongs to them. One at a time you hold the envelopes to your forehead and describe the owner from the 'vibrations' that your sensitive mind picks up from the objects, and then hand the correct object back to the correct person.

PREPARATION

The preparation for this trick takes about ten seconds. All you need are five envelopes but they need to be marked so that you can tell them apart. There are many different ways to mark the envelopes but the simplest is as follows. Place a pencil dot in the top left corner of the first envelope, the top right corner is marked for the second envelope. The third and fourth are marked in the bottom left and right corners respectively. The fifth envelope remains unmarked. Even if someone does notice the dot it is unlikely that they will realize what it is for.

PRESENTATION

After your introductory spiel about psychometry, ask for five volunteers to join you on the stage for a demonstration. Line them up across the stage and mentally number them from one to five. Explain that you want them to drop a personal item into an envelope and seal the envelope down. Hand out the envelopes so person number one gets the envelope marked in the top left corner and so on.

The envelopes are now collected and

mixed around so no-one knows who owns which envelope. It would be possible to look at the envelopes, locate the secret marks and hand them straight back to the rightful owner but this would not be very entertaining. You must now start acting to convince the audience that you are picking up vibrations. Take the first envelope and locate the secret mark so that you know who put the item in the envelope. Then start to describe the person, initially be very vague and then after a few introductory remarks be a little more precise about the owner. After you have 'divined' as much as you can from the vibrations, open the envelope and ask the owner of the item to step forward and claim it.

Here are some examples of what you might say as you hold the envelope to your forehead.

'This item belongs to a person who, I think is a man, yes, it definitely belongs to a man. Someone who enjoys watching sports' (a safe bet, most men enjoy watching sport!)'The person is quite tall and thin and has short dark hair.' (Tear open the envelope and take out the item). 'The item is a key, and I think it belongs to you, sir.' (Hand the item to the man you have just described and when he verifies that it is his, ask the audience to give him a round of applause as he sits down).

'This object belongs to someone who likes reading and is a fun-loving person, someone who enjoys life to the full. I get the impression that reading small print is a bit difficult.' (Say this if the owner wears glasses). 'I see someone with fair hair, another man I think, no, it's not a man it is a woman, (tear open the envelope) so this watch must be yours.' (Hand the watch to its owner).

You can use anything you know about the owners in your 'vague' descriptions. If they like fast cars you can say that they enjoy the feeling of speed, if they are wearing a badge that gives away a club they belong to, for example a rowing club sweatshirt, you might say that they like sport but that it is an unusual one, something to do with water, not swimming, but boating. Anything you can pick up on should be dropped casually into the descriptions.

When you get to the last two envelopes you need to take a slightly different approach. Have the two people standing either side of you and hold an envelope in each hand. As you describe the people either side of you, be indecisive about which envelope belongs to which person. Then, when you have finally felt enough of the vibrations, give the right envelope to the right person and ask them to check the contents and tell the audience whether or not you are correct.

Properly performed, this trick is a show stopper and has been performed in slightly different ways by mind readers all over the world. The key to making this trick great is not the method but the acting out of the scene. The audience must believe that it is not a trick but a genuine feat of psychometry.

CLIPPED PREDICTION

You hold a column from the local newspaper and tell the audience that it is a story about football, or whatever, and that you are going to use it in a mind reading experiment. Explain that you are going to move a pair of scissors up and down the column until someone shouts stop. Even when this is done you will then move the scissors again if the audience requests it. When everyone is happy, you cut through the column of print and a piece flutters to the floor. A member of the audience picks up the piece and concentrates on the first line of the clipping. You are able to read their mind and tell them exactly what they are thinking.

PREPARATION

Choose a suitable story from the paper and cut it out. The headline should be bold and the story should be fairly long (at least 15cm) and contain no words in bold type or lists, just a straight story. Separate the story from the headline and turn it round so that the story is upside-down. The end of the story will now be just below the headline and the start of the story at the bottom. Carefully glue it back onto the headline. Cut off the bottom line (the first line of the story) so that the story starts mid-sentence. Remember that sentence as it is the one that will be thought about by your volunteer.

The trick works because the audience member picks up the part of the story that has fluttered to the ground after it was cut. Everyone thinks that it is in the middle of the story but, thanks to your preparation, when they look at the top line of the paper they will be reading what was the bottom line of your upside-down column.

PRESENTATION TIPS

When working on a trick like this it is best to use a clipboard and a black marker pen to write down your thoughts as they come to you. Mind reading is not a science and does not always work exactly, so when reading a mind, make a few mistakes. Ask your volunteer to concentrate on the top line of the paper and as they do, write your thoughts on the clipboard. Take some time and pretend that you are having problems. Get them to concentrate harder. This is a great ruse as the audience will be more impressed when you eventually do get it right. When you are happy with your prediction ask the volunteer to read aloud the first line of the story. You can then turn round your clipboard and show that you are correct.

Above: The story is cut from the headline, turned upside down, and then glued back into position.

Right: From a distance it is impossible to notice the fact that the column of print is upside-down. The column can be cut anywhere and you will still be able to divine the words on the first line.

MONEY MAGIC

When people discover that you can do magic you will get a lot of funny requests. A father will ask you to make his children disappear, a wife may want you to make her husband go away. Some people might even suggest that you make yourself vanish. But the most popular request that I get is to conjure up some money. If I could do that I would be living in the West Indies and driving a Rolls Royce !

Money is an important part of our society, it is the oil that keeps the machinery functioning. Without money you would not have bought this book! Money has been around since the earliest civilizations found it better than bartering, and it is certainly easier to give change than it is to work out the exchange rates between goats and chickens.

Money can be fun for magicians,

imagine being able to make coins disappear in front of the cashier's eyes at the checkout till, or making a wad of paper money appear at your fingertips. With a lot of practice and a bit of luck you might one day be a professional magician and find yourself really making money by magic!

THE FRENCH DROP

Right: As the right hand covers the coin the left thumb is raised to let the coin drop back.

The French Drop is a move that will take a little practice to master but will enable you to make any small object disappear. Most of us have seen someone do this trick, it is probably the first trick you ever saw.

The coin starts in the left hand on the left side of the body – the eyes are on the coin.

The hands come together and the coin is 'taken' by the right hand – keep watching the coin.

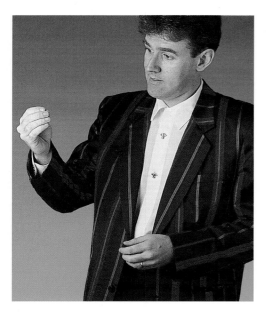

The eyes follow the coin as it is raised in the right hand.

Did you ever see someone take a coin and put it into his other hand, from there to vanish only to re-appear behind your ear. Well, to do that you must master the French Drop.

WHAT THE AUDIENCE SEE
From the point of view of a spectator a coin is taken in your left hand, placed into your right hand and from there it simply disappears. Notice in the picture sequence on the left that the coin starts at the left side of the body, moves to the centre where it is placed in the other hand, and is then taken off to the right side of the body in the right hand. Practise this simple exchange of the coin from one hand to the other a few times. Make sure that your eyes follow the position of the coin, this is actually a piece of misdirection as when you learn the next part of the move the coin will be retained in your left hand. If your eyes follow the coin then so will the eyes of the audience, they will not suspect you of cheating.

THE SECRET MOVE
The French Drop is the secret move by which you retain the coin in your left hand in the above sequence. It takes place at the moment the coin is transferred from one hand to the other (see picture centre left). From the very beginning, the coin is held in the left hand between fingers and thumb. As the hands come together, the thumb of the right hand goes behind the coin and the fingers cover the coin from

Above: The coin is caught in the finger palm position so the left hand can then hold the coin without anyone noticing

the front. As soon as the coin is hidden from view, the left thumb is raised a fraction and the coin falls back into the fingers of the left hand where it remains. (See Finger Palm page 67). The right hand mimes the action of taking the coin away. The left hand, still holding the coin loosely in the fingers, is casually dropped to your side.

PERFORMANCE TIP
There should be a time delay between the secret move and showing the coin has vanished or people might become suspicious and accuse you of cheating. Never rush to open your right hand, wait until the left hand (with the coin) has relaxed to your side. If you keep your eye on the place where the coin is meant to be and really believe in your mind that it is there, the audience will also believe it.

THE COIN FOLD

The magician borrows a coin from a member of the audience and slowly wraps it up in a piece of paper. The paper is visible at all times and the coin is clearly seen to be inside the folded paper. You can even see the outline of the coin if you look carefully at the little package. The spectators will be certain that they know where the coin is – but the magician quickly tears the paper package into tiny pieces and the coin has vanished.

PREPARATION

You will need a coin and a piece of paper about 10cm (4in) square. The diagram shows the positions of the folds that you are about to make. It may be helpful to pre-fold a piece of paper, as shown, to learn the trick. In performance there is no need to do this.

PERFORMANCE

The coin, which should be borrowed, is held against the paper slightly above the central position. Coin and paper should start off in the left hand with your left thumb holding the coin in position. Using the right hand, make the first fold as shown. Complete the fold and take the paper in your left hand ready for the next fold.

Next, you must fold the right side of the paper under the package and to do this use the fingers of your right hand. At the end of the fold take the package in your right hand.

This fold is almost identical to the second fold. You must now fold the left side of the paper under the package using the fingers of your left hand. The package is retained in the right hand in preparation for the last fold.

For the final fold turn the paper round and use the left hand to tuck the top of the package back and under. This will leave a secret opening that the coin can slip through. As soon as the opening is pointing downwards, gravity slides the coin out and into your waiting fingers which should be cupped and ready to steal the coin away. The package (now empty) is taken in the right hand and shown to the audience. The left hand (with the coin) is allowed to casually drop to your side. The paper package can now be torn up to show that the coin has vanished.

PERFORMANCE TIP

When you steal the coin out of the package remember to keep your eyes and your mind on where the coin should be, not where it really is.

Above: The first fold.

Right: The second fold.

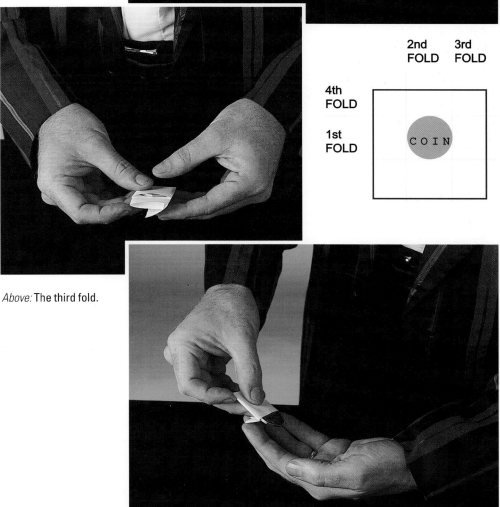

Above: The third fold.

Right: The final fold.

	2nd FOLD	3rd FOLD
4th FOLD		
1st FOLD	C O I N	

THE MISER'S DREAM

The Miser's Dream enables the performer to reach into mid-air and pluck a coin from nowhere, to reach behind a knee and find another one, to help himself to coins that are behind people's ears, under their lapels, in fact, everywhere you look you can find a coin. If I were a real magician this is a trick that I would like most to do. Unfortunately real magicians do not exist, so I have to keep pretending I can do it, and here is how you can pretend to do it too.

PREPARATION

To perform this trick you will need about ten coins all of the same size. Large silver coins are best as they are more visible than copper coins. One of the coins is gimmicked by glueing a loop of invisible thread or thin fishing line to one side. This is the coin that will keep appearing at your fingertips. You will also need a bucket to drop the coins in, a metal champagne bucket is ideal as it looks nice and showy and the coins make a chinking sound when they land in it.

There are two parts to this trick and you should practise each part separately before trying to do them together.

Left: The Gimmicked Coin – use invisible thread for the loop. String has only been used in the pictures to make the handling easy to see.

THE LEFT HAND

Take the stack of unprepared coins and hold them in your left hand, spread along the length of your fingers. Place the hand and the coins against the inside of the champagne bucket so that the left thumb is free to grip the outside of the bucket. You should be able to hold the bucket securely without using the fingers of your left hand.

Using your second finger slide the first coin free of your fingers and let it drop to the bottom of the bucket. The first and

Above: The coins in the left hand are spread along the fingers in preparation for taking hold of the bucket.

Above: The correct position of the hand and the bucket. You must be able to drop the coins singly and at the right moment.

third fingers are used to stop the other coins from moving about. Your audience should never be aware of the fact that a number of coins are held in this manner, so movement of these fingers should be kept to a minimum. You must practise this move until you can drop the coins, one at a time, into the bottom of the bucket. This move will be performed at the same time as you are pretending to drop a coin into the bucket with your right hand. The noise of the coin hitting the bottom of the bucket must be timed to match the dropping action of the right hand. Practise this by pretending to throw a coin into the air with your right hand, follow the imaginary coin with your eyes and pretend to catch it in the bucket. As the invisible coin lands in the bucket, drop a coin from your left fingers, the clink of the coin as it lands in the bottom of the bucket makes the illusion complete.

THE RIGHT HAND

The gimmicked coin is used in your right hand by looping the invisible thread over your thumb and holding the coin between your first finger and thumb. The back of your hand is towards the audience and the fingers are pointing slightly upwards. You are now going to drop the coin into the bucket, and as you do this the angle of your hand changes so the fingers are pointing slightly downwards. The moves you make must resemble gently throwing the coin into the bucket. Because of the thread looped over the thumb, the coin will hang in a position where it is hidden from the audience by the back of your hand.

To produce the coin, use the thumb to push it back up into the starting position. With this gimmick you can produce coins from mid-air or from under your arm, from the bottom of the bucket, or wherever you like.

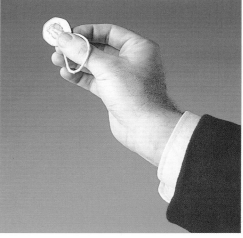

Above: Starting position, displaying the coin at your fingertips and showing it to the audience.

Above: After 'dropping the coin into the bucket' it hangs conveniently in your palm.

As a finale to The Miser's Dream you can produce a stream of coins from the elbow of a member of the audience. Place the bucket in your right hand (fingers inside the bucket) and shake it up and down to let the audience hear how much money you have found. This action will cause the coins to rise and fall and you will find it possible to catch some coins under your right fingers. At the same time, and using your left hand, bend the arm of a member of the audience to the position shown above. Transfer the bucket back to the left hand keeping the coins in the curled fingers of the right. Your right hand goes straight to the helper's elbow, gives it a shake and releases the coins, catching them in the bucket.

PUTTING IT ALL TOGETHER

The illusion of the Miser's Dream is created by combining the two moves described already so that the audience see you produce a coin and hear it as it is dropped into the bucket. The timing of the left hand is therefore critical. After the coin has been produced you bring your right hand to a position above the bucket and gently throw the coin into the bucket. The right hand must be close to the bucket as you make the throwing action or the audience may notice that the coin has been retained in your hand. By experimenting, you will soon learn the correct time to drop the coin so that the noise from the

bucket sounds as though it has come from a coin that you just threw in. When you have mastered the timing of the two moves, you are ready to start performing the trick.

In performance, you can move around the room grabbing coins from everywhere and dropping them in the champagne bucket. When producing coins from mid-air, it is important that you do a bit of mime. The first thing to do is pretend to see the coin floating in mid-air. Without taking your eyes off the spot where you imagine the coin to be, reach up with your right hand (the hand that contains the gimmicked coin) and quickly push the coin to your finger tips with your thumb.

Pause to let the audience see the coin, look at it and with an air of someone who is pleased with themselves, smile and drop the coin into the bucket. This can be repeated ad lib and get faster and faster until you have exhausted the supply of coins in your left hand. Between productions, you can shake the bucket a little to let the audience hear the coins. They will notice that the bucket is filling up by the difference in the sound. When you have run out of coins you can shake the bucket and catch a few under your left fingers and continue your productions. At the end of the trick the gimmicked coin can be really thrown up into the air and caught in the bucket.

MONEY FROM NOWHERE

The Miser's Dream is a trick where you produce coins but, with the rate of inflation on the rise, it would be better to produce paper money. So here is a trick where you do just that. After showing both of your hands empty you can produce a wad of bills big enough to make anyone's eyes pop out. This is a lot of fun if you are in a restaurant or a bar and it is your turn to buy the drinks. The only bad news about this feat of legerdemain is that it is only a trick. After mastering it you will not really be producing money from nowhere, you will be pulling it from the place where it was hidden moments before you do the trick. If you can't find eight treasury bills to practise with there is no need to worry. Cut some bill shaped pieces of newspaper and you will be ready to learn 'Money from Nowhere'.

PREPARATION
You will need about eight treasury bills of any denomination for this trick. The notes do not need to be all of the same value but should be similar in size or they are more difficult to handle. Roll the bills into a tight tube and place it on the inside of the crook of your left elbow (see below). The sleeve material of your shirt or jacket can now be pulled back a little to cover the roll of money. When you have loaded the money for this trick, you must remember that movement of your left arm is limited. If you drop your arm, the money may be

seen or slip from its hiding place and end up all over the floor – not such a good trick! Keep the arm bent at 90° at all times. This is made easy by holding a drink in your left hand. Now forget about the money and try to avoid spilling the drink and everything will be safe.

PERFORMANCE
To produce the money you need to practise the following moves so they look natural. You must avoid making a big deal of the fact that you are showing your hands empty even though that is what you *are* doing. Keep in your mind the fact that you are pulling up your sleeves and the moves will be a lot more natural.

The action of pulling up your right sleeve allows you to naturally show that the right hand is empty. Grasp the sleeve near to the inner elbow with your left hand (at roughly the same position as the notes are concealed in the left sleeve). The action of pulling up the right sleeve should be identical to the next action which is

pulling up the left sleeve. Practise this without the notes in position to get a natural feel to the move.

When you pull up the left sleeve the notes will naturally fall into your hand. You should not need to grab the notes as they will be right where you put your hand. Do not look to your elbow when pulling up your sleeve. The audience will look wherever you look, so do not draw their attention to the place where the secret move is happening.

When you have picked up the notes, bring your hands together and unroll the money. When you try this action you will find that the left arm will naturally cover the right hand (which now contains the money) giving extra cover to the subterfuge. Pulling up your sleeves is a natural action. No-one will suspect that that was how you got the roll of notes. Try not to rush the last action as any change in tempo will arouse suspicion. The whole sequence should be performed at a steady and even pace.

Above: Pull up the right sleeve and show the right hand empty.

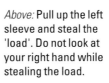

Above: Pull up the left sleeve and steal the 'load'. Do not look at your right hand while stealing the load.

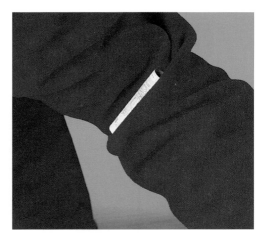

Left: The notes are hidden in the sleeve near the crook of the elbow, hide them by pulling back the sleeve and bending the arm.

Left: As you lift the notes from the fold in your jacket, the thumb goes under the notes and the fingers cover them from the audience's view.

64

THE TREASURY NOTE ROUTINE

For as long as money has existed, magicians have been borrowing it, loosing it, finding it, burning and restoring it. Anything that can be done has been done. But when it is your money that has been lost or destroyed you will be very keen for the trick to work. If it is a friend's money then you can relax and watch him worry about the final outcome of the trick. Borrowing a high denomination bank note adds a certain excitement to the trick, so always go for the biggest value note that you can manage.

In this version of the trick, a note is borrowed and a corner is torn off and given to your volunteer to keep. The note will now be easily identified at the end. The note is wrapped in a hanky and held firmly by its owner, magic salt is shaken over the note and the next moment it has vanished. The magician proudly announces that everything is under control and asks the volunteer to open the salt pot and look inside. What do you think he finds? Salt. This will cause much amusement to the spectators as your worried victim thinks that he is not going to get his note back. To make up for the unfortunate mishap, you offer your victim a Polo Mint (or Lifesaver), but before he takes the packet you snap it in half. Inside the sweets is a roll of paper which you unroll. It is a note with the corner missing. Ask to see the corner that was given to the volunteer at the start of the trick and you will see that they match exactly.

PREPARATION

You must prepare for this trick by tearing a corner off a note and putting it aside for later. Carefully open the end of a packet of Polo Mints or Lifesavers so that the holes through the sweets are exposed. Roll the bulk of the note into a tight tube and slide it into the centre of the packet of sweets. Re-seal the packet by folding the silver paper

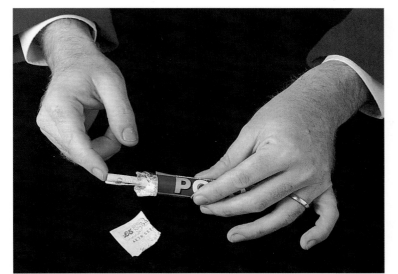

Roll the note into a tube and it will fit neatly inside the holes through the sweets

back into position. At the start of the trick, the Polos and the corner of the note should be in your left pocket. You will also need a salt pot, and a Devil's Hanky to make the borrowed note disappear, instructions on how to make and use one are on page 39.

PERFORMANCE

1. BORROWING A NOTE

The first stage of the trick is to borrow a treasury note that matches the one you have secretly loaded into the Polos. While your volunteer is hunting through his money put your hands in your pockets and get out the Polos and the corner of the note. Put the Polos on a table and retain the corner in the loosely curled fingers of the left hand (see Finger Palm page 67). By now your volunteer should have his note which you take with your right hand and

place into your left hand on top of the duplicate corner. The duplicate corner remains hidden from the audience while you tear the matching corner from the borrowed note. As you are doing this, tell the audience that the corner is a type of insurance and ask the spectator to look after it. As you say this you are going to switch the corners so that the volunter gets the corner from the note in the Polos.

2. THE SWITCH

After tearing the corner off the borrowed note you will have the corner in your right

Above: After the switch, the borrowed corner is hidden by raising your hand and holding the back of the note towards the audience.

Left: The duplicate corner is shown in the left hand in readiness for the switch. During performance, the corner would be completely hidden by the note.

4. THE FINALE

The note has vanished and you can proudly state that it has flown around the room and come to rest inside the salt pot. Give the pot to the volunteer and ask him to look inside and tell you what he finds. When he tells you that the salt pot contains nothing but salt you must look surprised and worried at the same time. The audience will enjoy the fact that the trick has gone wrong and your victim may be a little worried as well. Offer to make amends by giving him a packet of Polos. The Polos are worth a lot less than the note so he will probably not be too pleased. Try to convince him by telling him that the Polos are worth more than the note was, and when he has made it clear that he doesn't believe you, give him the Polos and ask him to snap them in half. He will be very surprised to find that inside the Polos is a rolled up note.

Unroll the note to show that a corner is missing from it. Retrieve the corner that

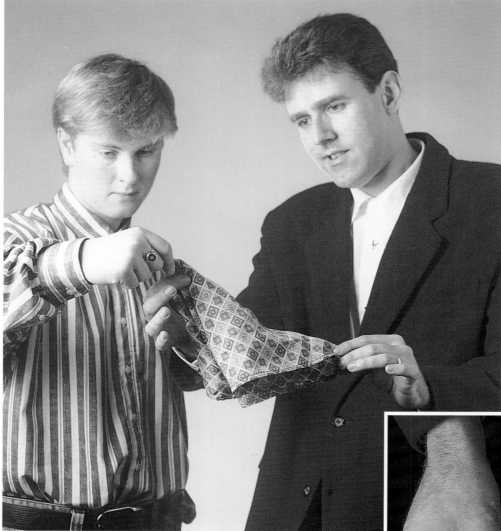

Above: The best way to vanish the note is to use a Devil's Hanky.

Right: At the finale of the routine check to see if the corner matches, you will find that it fits exactly.

hand and the duplicate corner and note will be in your left hand. The switch of the corners is made under the guise of swapping the note and the corner between hands. This is a very deceptive move as the audience is not aware of the duplicate corner. The borrowed corner is placed on top of the note and both are taken in the right hand, leaving the duplicate corner in the left hand. As your hands are separating, the left hand pushes the duplicate corner to your finger tips and the right hand turns the back of the note to the audience, concealing the extra corner. The duplicate corner is handed to the owner of the note for safe keeping and the borrowed note is folded into quarters. (This hides the torn corner in the folds of the note and keeps it safe. At a later date the note can be repaired with sticky tape).

3. THE VANISHING TRICK

To make the note disappear, we are going to use a Devil's Hanky. A description of the moves used for this trick can be found on page 39. The treasury note, now folded into quarters, is placed in the secret pocket of the hanky and given to the spectator to hold. Stress the fact that he can feel the note and ask him to hold it tight so as not to lose it. When the note is in the hanky you have done all the necessary moves to complete the trick so you can concentrate on building the suspense. Take out your magic salt and shake it on the hanky and on the count of three pull the hanky from the spectator's grip and show that the note has vanished.

your volunteer has been looking after and you will find that it not only matches but it fits exactly. Return the borrowed note to the spectator and take your well earned applause.

AFTERTHOUGHTS

Using the above method you can have the note appear almost anywhere. A favourite amongst magicians is to put the rolled up note inside a lemon. Use your imagination and see if you can find an original place to hide the duplicate note.

THE ONE HAND CHANGE

This is not a trick but a move which is used in a number of tricks. The Fortune Teller's Fiddle (page 68) is one such trick and some ideas are given for you to work on your own tricks using this move. The move is designed to help you secretly and silently switch one coin for another, but the same move is used for switching ping-pong balls, bits of paper or any small objects.

Right: The Finger Palm. Used for retaining small objects in the hand. With the back of the hand to the audience and relaxed fingers, the hand looks quite empty.

STAGE 1

At the start of this move, one coin (copper) is held between the thumb and first finger. The second coin (silver) is held in the Finger Palm. The copper coin is held so that it will balance on the first finger when the thumb is removed.

STAGE 2

Raise the thumb and balance the copper coin on the tip of your first finger. Bend the first finger back and push the copper coin into the thumb in the thumb palm position (see illustration). It can be gripped quite lightly in this position without slipping. The silver coin does not move in this first stage of the One Hand Change.

STAGE 3

Without loosing the grip on the copper coin in the thumb palm position, the tip of the thumb is lowered onto the centre of the silver coin. At the same time the fingers are straightened in readiness for the last stage.

STAGE 4

To complete the moves, we need to get back to the starting position with the coins transposed. This is accomplished by pushing the silver coin towards the tip of the first finger with the thumb. As the coin slides past the second finger and onto the first finger, the other fingers are curled back to pick up the coin from the thumb palm and place it in the finger palm position.

The first time you try this, the coins are likely to fall between your fingers but with a little practice it will become smooth. The whole move takes a split second and you can practise while watching T.V. When you have it mastered you can go on to learning the move with folded treasury notes, ping-pong balls and keys. Then look at the next page for a few suggestions for tricks with the One Hand Change.

Left: Starting position for the One Hand Change.

Right: Second position for the One Hand Change.

Left: Third position for the One Hand Change.

Right: Final position (coins changed places).

THE FORTUNE TELLER'S FIDDLE

This trick is a story trick that shows how people can be conned into losing money, and teaches them to be more careful. The cover for the sleight of hand is totally logical so it is a very convincing piece of magic. Here is the story as I tell it but always personalize a story by putting yourself or someone you know into it.

THE STORY

When my grandfather was a young man he went to a travelling fair. He had won a coconut on the coconut shy, got merry on the merry-go-round and was wearing an awful tie because the man couldn't guess his weight! He was about to leave when a gypsy fortune-teller attracted his attention and he decided that he would like to take a look into his future.

The gypsy showed him into her caravan, sat him down, and asked him questions about his life and his dreams. She then gazed into a crystal ball and told him his fortune. Just before he left, she made him a magic charm for good luck.

The magic charm was made like this. He was told to take a treasury note, the biggest he had, and screw it up into a ball. The gypsy took the note and covered it with a hanky, and tied it up with a piece of string. This little package was to bring him good luck but only if it was kept safely tied up for seven days and seven nights.

My grandfather was a superstitious man so he followed her instructions. Seven days and seven nights he waited and when he finally opened the package he found a ball of worthless paper. He rushed back to the fairground but by now the fair had gone and his money was lost. But the story does have a happy ending. There was a young girl in the field and she was crying. She too had been caught by the fortune-teller's fiddle, and that girl became my grandmother. Maybe the fortune-teller brought them both good luck after all.

THE METHOD

At the start of this trick you will need a treasury note, a hanky, a ball of paper and a rubber band(this should be in your right pocket). When you come to the point in the story where you make the magic charm, suit the actions to the words. Hold the ball of paper loosely and secretly in the fingers of the right hand (the Finger Palm position). Screw up the note into a ball in your left hand and place it at the fingertips of your right hand. You are now ready to execute the One Hand Change. Cover your right hand with the hanky and do the change, this will bring the ball of paper to the tips of the fingers and the note to the finger palm. Take the ball of paper through the hanky with your left hand (leaving the note behind) and place your right hand into the right pocket. Leave the note in the pocket and bring out the band to wrap around the hanky. The charm is now made and the note has been secretly switched out.

OTHER USES FOR THE ONE HAND CHANGE

Here are a few ideas that use the One Hand Change:

Have a coin marked with a sticker which can be signed and execute the One Hand Change to switch the coin for a duplicate. The marked coin can then be put aside for later discovery while you make the duplicate coin vanish using the Devil's Hanky or the French Drop. The marked coin could be produced from inside a bread roll (see Coin from Bread Roll) or from a sealed envelope or anywhere.

A large denomination note could be switched for a small denomination note during a money trick giving an extra surprise when the note is unfolded.

A napkin could be screwed into a ball and when unscrewed magic writing could be found to have appeared on the napkin, such as the name of a chosen card or someone's phone number.

The One Hand Change could be used in a spooky ghost trick to make a mystic message appear on a piece of paper that has been folded up.

Put your imagination to work and see if you can come up with a new trick all of your own that uses the One Hand Change.

HEADS OR TAILS

This is one of the simplest coin tricks to perform and yet it is still totally baffling to the spectators. Five coins are borrowed and placed on the table. While your back is turned, you instruct someone to turn over coins two at a time, and as many times as they like; this can be done silently so that you are not aware of how many coins have been turned. You then tell a member of the audience to cover one of the coins with a beer mat or a playing card. You turn round and correctly divine whether the covered coin is heads or tails.

METHOD

The secret is so simple that it fools everybody. Try this for yourself. Put five coins on the table, making sure that there is an even number of heads. Turn the coins two at a time and you will notice that it is impossible to change the fact that there is an even number of heads. Try it again with an odd number of heads and there will always be an odd number as long as you turn two coins at a time. This is the system on which the trick is based.

When the coins are first placed on the table, remember if there is an odd or an even number of heads. Then turn your back and go through the turning procedure, making sure that coins are turned two at a time. Then ask your volunteer to cover one of the coins. Emphasize that it could be a head or a tail and you have no way of knowing which. Turn back and look at the coins. If the original head count was even and there is still an even number of heads on view then the covered coin is a tail; if the number of heads on view is odd then it is a head. If the original head count gave you an odd number and you still see an odd number of heads then the covered coin is a tail; if you see an even number of heads then the covered coin is a head.

This may seem a little complicated to remember but after trying it you will see that it is easy to remember. Especially when you look at the table below.

BEFORE	AFTER	RESULT
Even	Even	Tail
Even	Odd	Head
Odd	Odd	Tail
Odd	Even	Head

ROPEY TRICKS

Every rope has two ends and a middle, but give it to a magician and something strange begins to happen. Magicians love to do tricks with everyday objects, and as all you need for some tricks is a piece of rope or string, you can be ready to perform at the drop of a . . . rope!

The best rope to use for most of the following tricks should be of soft cotton. It is available from most good hardware stores and usually comes with a stiffer central core which must be removed for our purposes. This is easily accomplished by cutting the rope to the desired length and gently pulling it out. The result is a much more pliable rope that will make the tricks a lot easier to do. Have fun with the following tricks, I know I have.

THE STRING AND STRAW

This is a simple yet effective trick that can be performed almost anywhere. You will need a drinking straw and a piece of string about 45cm (18in) long. The string is threaded through the straw and folded in half and the centre of the straw is then snipped away cutting the string in two. The magician (that's you) can then restore the string back to its original state.

This trick will amuse spectators if, instead of string, you borrow a shoelace and proceed to cut it in half! You can then pretend that the trick has gone wrong before you restore the lace, to the relief of your victim.

PREPARATION

Any piece of string or shoelace will do for this trick as they do not need to be prepared. The straw, however, needs a little work. With a sharp modelling knife, cut a slit about 8cm (3in) long in the straw (see illustration). Be careful to only cut one side. This preparation will not be noticed by your audience.

Above: Carefully cut through half of the straw. The slit should be about 8cm (3in) long.

PERFORMANCE

Thread the lace through the straw and fold it in half. Make sure that the slit in the straw is on the inside of the fold.

When the straw has been completely folded in half, place it into your left hand and, with your right first finger and thumb, gently pull on the lace where it enters the straw. This will pull the centre

Right: With the lace threaded through fold the straw in half. Make sure the cut is on the inside of the fold

Below: Exposed view pulling the lace into the slit. During performance the straw should be folded fully in half.

Below: cut the straw close to but above the lace

Below: with a gentle rubbing action of the fingers you can magically weld the lace back together

of the lace into the slit and thus avoid any damage when you snip the straw. To show things clearly, the straw is slightly 'open' in the picture, but in performance, the straw would be fully folded in half.

The lace is now clear of the 'fold' in the straw so you can safely cut it away and the audience will think you have cut the lace in pieces. The best place to make the cut is 0.5cm (³⁄₈in) above the place where the lace goes through the slit.

To restore the lace, carefully straighten out the lace, make a magic pass with your hands and you can pull it free of the two pieces of straw and return it to its rightful owner.

THE GENIE'S BOTTLE

This is the story of a magic bottle which is the home of a tiny genie. He is not very powerful but, for his size, he is quite strong. If you place the end of a rope in the bottle and speak to him in his own language, he will hold on to it, and not let go. He is so strong that if you hold the rope and let the bottle hang he will still not release his grip on the rope. If you tug hard enough, you may be able to get him to let go. But no-one else will be able to do it – well that's probably because they do not speak Genie!

PREPARATION

For this trick you will need a little rubber ball. This can be made with a modelling knife from an eraser. Cut a cube out of the eraser and then trim away at the edges until it is roughly ball shaped. This ball must be kept secret from the spectators.

You will also need an opaque bottle, the one I am using is a brass vase, and a piece of rope that is almost the diameter of the bottle-neck.

PERFORMANCE

At the start of this trick, the ball is already in the vase/bottle. Take the rope and as you tell the story of the genie, drop the end of it into the top of the bottle. Invert the bottle and the ball will fall into the position shown, locking the rope in position. If the rope does not lock you will need a larger ball or a thicker piece of rope.

As you continue the story, you invert the bottle and show it hanging on the rope. If the ball is the correct size the bottle will hang firmly and you will be able to gently swing the bottle from side to side as much as you like.

To remove the rope, make a fist around the neck of the bottle, with the opening in the centre of your fist. Hold the bottle so it is horizontal and pull the rope firmly. The ball will come out of the bottle and end up in your hand and the rope will now be free. You can give the rope and the vase to someone else but without the ball they will not be able to duplicate your actions.

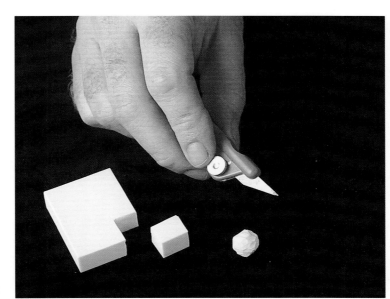

Left: Making the rubber ball – take care with the modelling knife, these blades are very sharp.

Right: A clear bottle has been used to show the working of the trick. For performance, an opaque bottle or a brass vase should be used.

Left: Stealing the ball from the vase before handing it out for examination. Pull the rope and the ball should pop into your hand. Using a heavy brass vase adds to the impact of the trick.

RAPID RING RELEASE

Two pieces of rope are tied onto a magic wand and onto these are threaded two rings. Another knot is tied in the ropes ensuring that the rings cannot slip off. A quick wave of the magic wand makes the knots disappear and the rings are free of the rope. A modern matter through matter miracle!

PREPARATION

There is no secret preparation for this trick, it can be performed with borrowed items. You will need a magic wand (a chop-stick or a pencil will do), two pieces of rope about 60cm (24in) long – long shoe laces or string work just as well – and a couple of finger or key rings.

PERFORMANCE

Get a volunteer to hold the end of the magic wand and drape the two ropes over it. These are then tied in a single knot, as shown, and pulled tight. In this position the wand will not slip out, so get your helper to hold the ends of the ropes. If you look carefully at the way the ropes are tied, you will see that the helper is holding the two ends of one rope in each hand whereas he thinks he is holding one end of each rope in each hand. This is the reason the rings eventually fall off the rope. You now ask to borrow a couple of rings; finger rings, key rings, any type of ring will do. One ring is then threaded onto each of the double ends of the ropes and along it and slipped right up to the magic wand.

Your helper will hold the ends of the ropes most of the way through the trick so that he will be certain that you do not slip the rings off the ends of the ropes. Just to make sure that this is impossible, take a single rope from each of his hands and tie a single knot around the rings.

To effect the release, all you have to do is slide the wand out of the knot. However, it looks more effective if you do it in the following manner. Take hold of the rings and remove the wand – holding the rings will ensure the knot (really a slip knot) does not unravel too soon.

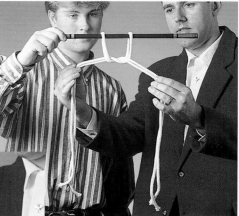

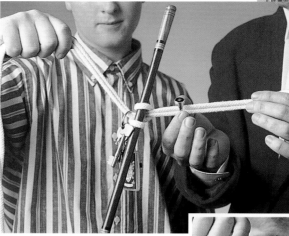

Above: The secret of the trick is in the way that this knot is tied. After the knot is pulled tight the wand will not slip out.

Left: Make sure both ends of the rope go through the ring.

Right: By now it looks impossible to release the rings.

Below: Pulling the wand out of the knot will free the rings but to make it more magical, hold onto the knot for a moment before the release.

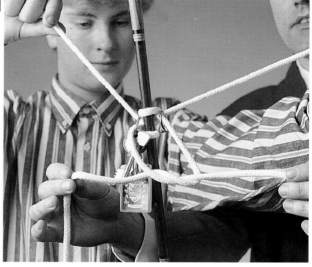

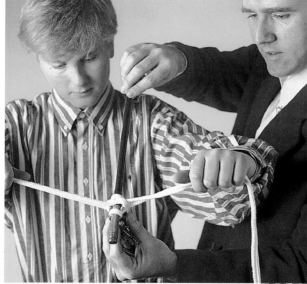

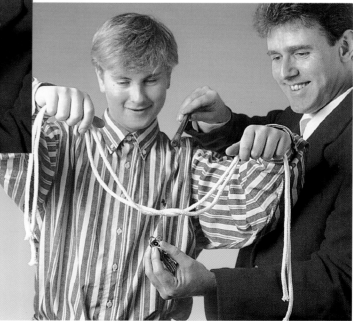

Right: Touch the knot with the wand to make it unravel 'by magic'.

THE CUT & RESTORED ROPE

This is a magic classic. No matter how often people see it performed, it is still a miracle. It is not the easiest of tricks to learn but with a little practice you will soon be amazing people with your magical powers. All you need is a piece of rope and a pair of scissors. Soft cotton rope or pyjama cord works best and is easy to cut. It is possible to do the trick with string but you will find it a little fiddly.

PERFORMANCE

Hold one end of the rope in your left hand as shown. At all times during this first move keep the back of your left hand to the audience. With your right hand, grasp the middle of the rope and start to raise it.

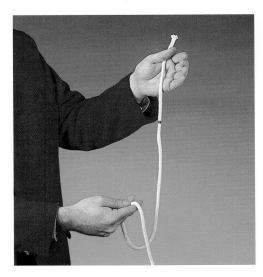

Above: The starting position – not the audience's view.

Note that the right thumb is on top and your first two fingers are underneath the centre of the rope, and that the fingers are pointing slightly upwards.

As you raise your right hand, grip the rope about 8cm (3in) below the left hand (where marked) between the first two fingers of that hand. As soon as you have the rope held between your fingers, push the loop of rope held by the thumb off the end of your fingers and continue to raise your right hand. Note that the fingers of the right hand are now pointing slightly downwards.

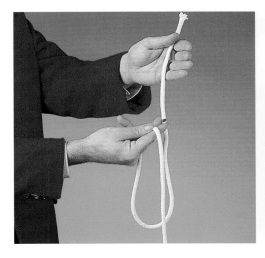

Above: Grip the rope between two fingers before pushing the loop free.

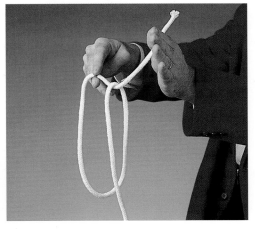

Above: The looped rope before you transfer it into the left hand.

Raise the loop that you are holding in your right hand and place it into your left hand. The left thumb grips the loop which should protrude by about 5cm (2in) above your left hand. This action should be performed smoothly and with no hesitation when you switch your finger positions to make the loop. To the audience it should look as if you have simply picked up the centre of the rope and placed it in your other hand. The motion of your right hand should be a straight line from the point where you first picked up the centre of the rope to the point where the loop was placed in the other hand.

The secret switch, detailed above, should leave the place where the loops intersect hidden in your left hand. If this intersection is not concealed then the right-hand fingers must grip the rope a little nearer the left hand.

This is the finishing position of the ropes before you cut at the loop. If you look carefully you will see that by cutting

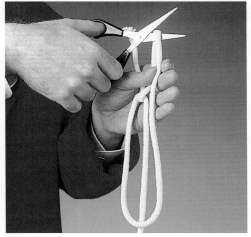

Above: Making the cut through the top loop only cuts of a short length.

rope in the loop you are only cutting a short piece off the end of the rope and not actually cutting it in half.

The above 'move' takes a little practice to perfect but it is well worth it. The rest of the trick is a lot easier as all you have to do now is cut and restore the rope. Remember that the move you have just done is not the trick but the means by which it is achieved, so do it in a casual manner. The trick does not really start until you actually cut the rope.

When the hard part is done, concentrate the audience's attention and

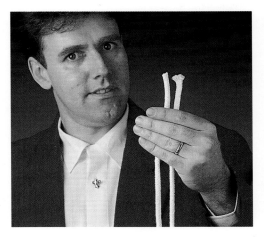

Above: The short rope is looped through the long rope, the hand covers the join. It looks like two long ropes.

cut the rope. After snipping through it at the top of the loop, let the end nearest the tips of your fingers fall. To the audience it will look as if you are now holding two pieces of rope of approximately equal lengths. In reality, you have a short piece looped through a long piece.

There are a number of different ways to restore the rope. Practise each one and choose the one that is most natural to you.

RESTORATION 1

Tie the ends of the short loop of rope into a knot around the long piece of rope. You can now display the two ropes tied together quite freely. If you performed the move described above smoothly, no-one will suspect that all is not as it seems. Hold one end of the rope in your right hand and with your left hand, wrap the rope around your right hand. As you come to the knot, simply slide it along the rope (keeping it in your left hand). When you get to the end off the rope the knot will fall off and you can steal it away in your left hand. To dispose of the knot, reach into your pocket for some magic dust and leave the knot there. You can now sprinkle the dust on the rope and unwrap it to show the knot has disappeared. The rope can now be handed around for examination.

RESTORATION 2

Take the scissors and snip away the ends cutting 2cm (¾in) at a time and letting the ends fall to the floor. When you have snipped away at the small loop till it has all gone, you can show the rope back in one piece. It can then be used for another trick such as the rapid ring release.

RESTORATION 3

This is the simplest of all the restorations and probably the most effective. It does, however, have the disadvantage that you cannot give the rope out for examination at the end.

With the right hand, take hold of either end of the long rope so that the rope goes into the top of your fist (the thumb end) but does not stick out at the bottom. Raise your right hand and grab one of the ends of the short rope from your left hand so that it is sticking out of the bottom of your fist. The long rope entering the top of your hand should line up with the short rope sticking out the bottom. Release your grip on the rope with your left hand and the rope will look as if it has been restored.

STRETCHING THE ROPES

If after cutting the ropes you find one rope looks longer than the other you might like to try the following.

After displaying the rope, apparently cut in half in your left hand, pick up the ends of the long rope and hold them in your right hand in a similar manner. With your two hands side by side the loops

Above: Cut away the small piece of rope, letting the waste drop to the floor, and you will be left with one long rope.

Left: Unbeknown to the audience there are two ropes, one long and one short, the join is held in the right hand.

between your hands will now hang at different heights. Make a sharp tugging action by pulling your hands away from each other (being careful not to let go of

anything as this will give the game away). The place where the ropes loop together will slip so the ropes now appear to be the same length.

74

ROPE THROUGH NECK

WARNING Do not perform tricks like this in front of young children as they may try to copy you and harm themselves.

This is a quick trick with an element of danger, so performed at the right time it can be very effective. The magician takes a length of rope and wraps it around his neck. One sharp tug and the rope passes straight through – to the relief of all who are watching. Take care when performing this trick and make sure you learn it thoroughly. The trick looks more effective with a long scarf but for reasons of clarity it is shown using a piece of rope. Any scarf or rope will do but it will need to be about 2 metres (6½ft) long.

PERFORMANCE

Drape the rope around your neck and take hold of it in the following manner. The thumbs go behind the rope but they do not grip it. The rope to your left is actually gripped with your right hand first and second fingers and the rope to your right is gripped the same way by your left hand.

Above: Both hands move left, but do different jobs.

Note: the left hand is above the right hand. Both hands now move at the same time toward the left and up around the head but they are doing different jobs. The left hand firmly grips a loop of the rope on the right side of your body and takes it to the left side of your neck. The right hand loosely takes the rope from the left side of your body and takes it right over and around your head.

Keeping hold of the loop in your left hand, slide the rope around your neck so the loop is brought to the back of your neck.

This whole movement is carried out in one smooth continuous action and should look as though you are simply wrapping the rope around your neck.

Above: Wrap the rope around the loop behind your neck. This is a view the spectators should not see.

By bending your head slightly backwards you will be able to keep the loop in position with your neck and safely let go. It should be reasonably tight around your neck without cutting off the air supply!

Take hold of one end in each hand and take up the slack. Do not pull it too tight or the loop will slip and be released before time. It is best to tighten the muscles of the neck and use your acting ability to feign pain as you pretend to pull. All it then takes is to relax and straighten up your head, the loop slips out of the rope and the rope frees itself from your neck. The last action should be a quick tug and the audience will see the rope pass through your neck.

Below: Act up the pain before the final tug.

Above: Begin with the thumbs behind the rope, which is gripped between two fingers of the opposite hand.

THE ONE-HANDED KNOT

This is not so much a trick as a neat piece of juggling which will give the impression of great skill. The best bit is that it is really very easy to do. What you are going to do is hold a piece of rope in one hand and, with a quick flip of the wrist, a knot appears tied in the rope. This trick can be performed equally well with a neck tie or a twisted handkerchief but has been shown here with a rope which is the easiest way to practise it.

PERFORMANCE

STAGE 1

A piece of rope about 60cm (24in) long is draped in the crook between finger and thumb of your right hand as shown. The tip of your little finger (pinkie) is used to catch one end of the rope and pull it away from the other end. Note the slight upward angle of the fingers.

Above: The placing of the rope to start the knot.

STAGE 2

Your hand now revolves in an anti-clockwise direction and your first and second fingers quickly grip the rope (it has been marked for clarity). The place where the rope is gripped is the spot that you can comfortably reach. Note that during this twist the fingers are now pointing slightly downwards. This helps the next part of the move which involves slipping the part of the rope which crosses the back of your hand down over your fingers and free from your hand, thus forming the knot.

STAGE 3

The hand is now turned back to its original position and the loop is slipped off the back of the hand. This is easier if you give the whole movement a downwards flick as soon as you have grabbed the rope in Stage 2 and as you proceed to Stage 3, jerk the fingers upwards, pulling the end of the rope through the loop.

STAGE 4

Continue the upwards movement and the knot will form and tighten. The whole movement lasts a split second and looks very impressive. If you find it difficult to pull the end through the loop, it is probably too long and you will need to adjust your starting position – try a little less rope trailing behind your hand and start again.

When you have mastered it with a rope try it with a handkerchief.

Left: Turning your hand, with the rope lodged between your fourth and little finger, you grip down the other end of the rope.

Below: The loop is slipped off the back of the hand to form the knot.

Below: Bringing the hand upwards, with the loop free and only the upper part of the rope between your fingers tightens the knot.

THE INDIAN ROPE TRICK

One of the mysteries of magic is the Indian rope trick. The story tells of an Indian fakir who would stand in a clearing and throw a rope into the air. By his magic powers, the rope would stiffen and stand upright and a small child would quickly climb up the rope and disappear. Many people have re-created the trick on stage but no-one has ever succeeded in performing the trick in the open air. Most people belief the trick is a fairy tale, part of Indian folklore, or at best a wildly exaggerated story. Because of that story the idea of a rope standing upright and defying gravity has a strange fascination for most people and this is a simple way of reproducing the effect.

PREPARATION

You will need a piece of rope about 1 metre (39in) in length. Most rope tricks can be done with any rope but this trick needs a rope that has a hollow core, a space through the centre of the rope. Into this space you push a piece of solder that is a little less than half the length of the rope.

Above: A piece of solder is pushed into the rope to provide the stiffening.

Solder is very flexible but is stiff enough to give the rope the rigidity needed to perform this trick. You must remember not to hand the rope out for examination before or after this trick.

PERFORMANCE

With your right hand, hold the rope in the centre and let the two ends drop down either side as shown. At the moment the

Above: Start the trick with the stiff end of the rope hanging from your little finger.

stiff end (the end with the solder in it) is to your right (the pinkie end of your hand). Pick up the loose end of the rope and attempt to balance it, you will fail and the rope will fall back down. This failure emphasizes to the audience that the rope is 'unprepared'. Drop your hand and the rope down to your side and explain that the Indian who taught you the trick wasn't a good teacher, or you were not a good learner! While talking, turn the rope around in your hand so that the stiff part of the rope is now at the top of your hand (the thumb end).

Above: Holding the stiffened end, the rope stays horizontal.

With your left hand, pick up the stiff end of the rope and hold it parallel to the ground. Change your grip with your right hand so the part of the rope containing the solder is between your fingers. To do this, simply slide your hand a little way along the rope. Gently let go of the end and the rope will mysteriously stay in position. You may want to wave your hand above and below the rope to show that there are no invisible strings holding it up.

Above: With the stiff end at the top, the rope stays vertical.

Take the stiff end and raise it up so that the rope is vertical. Again, carefully let go and the rope will stay suspended. When the applause dies down (!) you take the rope at the top with your left hand and using your right, you wrap the rope around your hand and toss it aside. Because the solder is very pliable you will find that you can carry out this last action very easily and the fact that you have you have tampered with the rope will go unnoticed.

NOTE : Solder is available in different thicknesses. Generally the thinner the better, but experiment to find the right thickness of solder for the weight of the rope that you are using.

CHINESE HANDCUFFS

This trick has an unusual name but it does not use handcuffs, and as far as I am aware, it is not Chinese. But it is a great trick. It is a simple release that can be a real reputation maker. Perform it well and people will be talking about you for a long time. Your wrists are tied together and a long rope is threaded between your hands. It is obviously impossible to escape from the long rope, but in a split second the rope seems to pass right through your wrists.

PERFORMANCE

You will need a piece of elastic bandage about 50cm (20in) long and a 3-metre (10ft) length of rope. And a member of the audience to tie you up.

After having everything examined, you ask to have your wrists tied with the bandage – get it tied as tightly as possible.

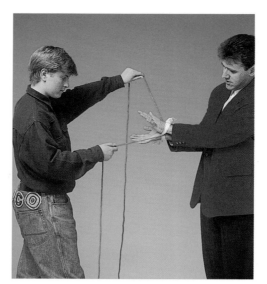

Above: A long piece of rope is threaded through your arms.

Right: As soon as the loop is large enough, slip it over one of your hands.

Below: A sharp tug will release you from the rope.

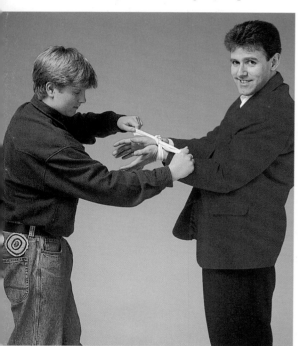

Above: First the wrists are tightly bound together.

You need very little slack in the bandage to do the release and because it is elasticated it is almost impossible to tie elastic bandage tightly.

The long length of rope is then fed down between your arms and your assistant, who takes the ends of the rope, walks away from you until the rope is

tight. The first few times you do this trick I suggest you have your hands covered with a head scarf. As your speed increases you can do it without a cover.

TO MAKE THE RELEASE

By pressing your wrists together and moving them back and forwards against each other you will be able to work a loop of rope through the bandage.

Continue the action until the loop is large enough to slip the fingers of either hand through the loop.

As you can see in the photo, by passing the hand through the loop, the rope is now only held by the loop tucked under the bandage. One sharp tug and you will be free.

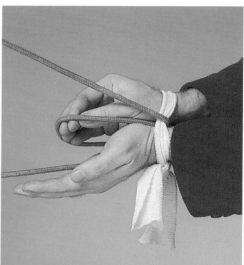

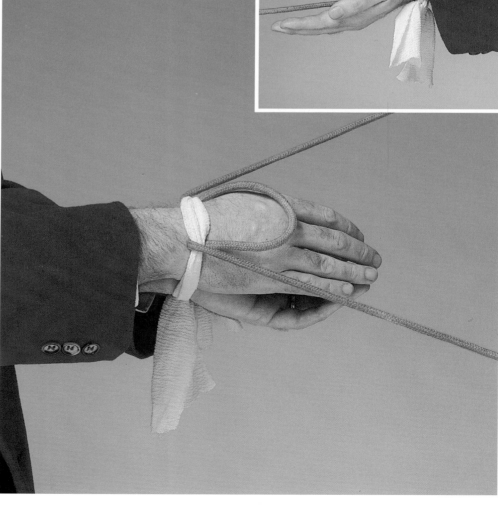

ROPE THROUGH BODY

To do this trick you will need two pieces of rope, each one about 2 metres (6½ft) in length. The ropes are wrapped and tied around your body and with one sharp tug they pass straight through and you are free, to the surprise and amazement of any onlookers. If you feel inclined, you can perform this trick on someone else, or have two people standing each side of you to pull the ropes.

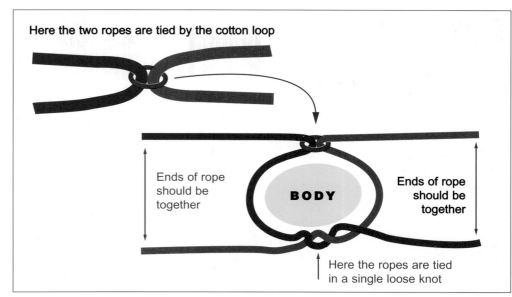

Here the two ropes are tied by the cotton loop

Ends of rope should be together

BODY

Ends of rope should be together

Here the ropes are tied in a single loose knot

PREPARATION

Fold the two ropes in half and tie them together with a loop of cotton. It is best to use a colour that matches the rope in case anyone catches a glimpse of it.

When the ropes have been prepared, place them in a box or bag so that when you begin to perform the trick they will be in a position to be picked up with the cotton hidden in the palm of your hand.

Above: The two ropes are linked with cotton at their centres.

Below: Hold the ropes to hide the link.

Right: Knots are tied in front as shown in the diagram above.

PERFORMANCE

By holding the ropes, as shown, it will look as though the two ropes are both passing through your hand rather than being folded in half. Pass the looped part of the ropes behind your back and bring the ends of the rope to each side of your body. Make sure you keep your back (and the part of the ropes tied by the cotton) out of sight of the audience.

Take a single piece of rope from each hand and tie a single knot in front of your body. The rope from the left goes through the knot and on to your right hand. The rope from the right goes to the left hand. The drawing should make the positions of the ropes clear and you will see that it is only the thin cotton that holds them in position.

When you are in this position, a sharp tug will release the ropes from your body. You might use two volunteers to hold on to the ends and then, on the count of three, they can pull on the ropes. Using members of the audience to participate in tricks like this makes them more theatrical. Don't let them pull on the ropes too soon because the ropes will fall free from your body and you will loose the big finish.

AN ALTERNATIVE PRESENTATION

Another way to present this effect is to slip the ends of the rope down the sleeves of a jacket, carefully keeping the cotton loop in the centre.

Above: Ropes threaded through jacket sleeves. Different coloured ropes have been used for clarity. In performance the ropes are identical.

Put the jacket on and you will have two pieces of rope coming out of each sleeve.

Take one rope from each sleeve and tie them in a single knot and you will end up in the position shown above. If two members of your audience pull on the ends, the cotton will break and the ropes will look as though they have passed through your jacket and through you as well!

Putting on an Act

Being able to do a magic trick is one thing, the ability to perform it is quite another. You must now learn to perform the tricks so that the audience will believe that what you are doing is magic. Always remember that your audience want to be entertained.

A simple trick, well performed, will be much better received than a complex one where you have to concentrate on the method rather than the presentation. It's not what you do but the way that you do it that really counts. It is much better to concentrate on a few tricks and really master them than to learn twenty tricks and not manage to entertain.

The first stage in putting an act together is to work out your character – a magician is an actor playing the part of a magician. The traditional magician is seen dressed in a dinner jacket or wearing top hat and tails, presenting an infallible air of having complete control over the objects and people that he is manipulating. Many modern magicians have left this style behind, presenting themselves as comedy magicians, relying as much on their patter as on their magic. Then there is the silent magician, performing his magic to music, be it in a comedy or a straight act. Your character will depend on a number of things: your natural looks, your patter ability, your clowning ability, your audience, etc. The most important thing is to experiment and develop your act. There is no such thing as the perfect act, so always keep working on improving it. When you have decided on your character you must then dress to fit. The clothes you wear when performing should be clean and smart as this is the first impression that the audience will have of you, and first impressions last.

The next job is to decide on the tricks that you are going to perform. You should start off with something snappy that will grab the attention of the audience, then move into the main part of your act, remembering to include as much variety as possible (people will not relish ten card tricks), and build up to a strong finish. Remember to enjoy yourself and do not rush through your act – look at your audience and keep smiling. If you enjoy performing, the audience will enjoy watching you.

You will always need to tailor your performance to suit your audiences, so here are some hints and tips for certain groups.

MAGIC FOR CHILDREN

This is great fun if you can play the part of the clown. You don't need to dress as a clown, but be zany in your performance. Do only simple and colourful magic. Good routines for children are the Change Bag Routine, Cut and Restored Rope, Productions etc. A lot of fun can be had if you misname colours and play the 'fool' in the best sense of the word. Let the children catch you out and then fool them with some magic.

FAMILY AUDIENCES

This is the best kind of audience for a magician and give the most scope. I favour a light comedy approach using as much audience participation as possible. Good routines would include the Treasury Note Routine, Mind Reading and Mathemagics, the Miser's Dream etc. The magic should be simple enough for the younger members and fun for the adults. Use some childern as volunteers – it charms the adults.

STREET SHOWS

When performing in the open air you should aim to be as big as possible. Escapes are always good as the challenge angle is exciting to watch. Illusions are also good, but watch for people standing behind you who could see how the trick is done.

WHERE TO PERFORM

Children's parties are a good start. Friends welcome you with open arms when you volunteer to entertain at little Johnny's birthday party! The best ages are between four and eight; any younger and they don't always follow, any older and they do not believe in magic and tell you so in no uncertain terms!

If you do not feel that you want to entertain children (and many people find it impossible) you will need to look for a family audience. This is easy to find at any social gathering in churches or in clubs; it is up to your ingenuity to find an audience. When you have done a few shows you will find that people will hear about you and search you out. If they don't, then you need to do some work on your act!

Another good place to try out your act is in the talent shows which are held in local pubs, bars and clubs all over the country. Never enter a talent competition expecting to win; just try to entertain your audience and gain experience. If they do not like you, do not take it personally. Any professional entertainer has 'died' many times; it is an occupational hazard that you just have to get used to.

A good way to improve your act is to show it to other magicians. There are clubs all over which welcome new members, but you will have to track them down. Try calling your local children's entertainer, who may be able to point you in the right direction. Most magicians are connected to the following two magic clubs. Both publish magazines which will keep you in touch with events and new developments in magic and who is doing what.

The Magic Circle

Probably the most famous magic club in the world, but very exclusive. The Circle has a vast library and a museum of magic and its history that is available to members. It meets every Monday evening, but is strictly members only. Write for details, enclosing a stamped addressed envelope to:
Mr. C. Pratt (Hon Secretary), 13 Calder Avenue, Brookmans Park, Herts, AL9 7AH

The International Brotherhood of Magicians

The IBM is the largest magic club and has rings all over the world. Many organize conventions, held annually. These are exciting events where you can see great magicians, exchange ideas and buy new props from dealers in magic.

In America, there are rings in many different States. Contact the IBM's headquarters to locate your nearest ring

International Brotherhood of Magicians, P O Box 227, Kenton, Ohio 43326

The Secretary of the British Ring is:
H. J. Atkins, Kings Garne, Fricham Court, Fricham, Lyndhurst, Hampshire, SO43 7HH